Connecting
with
Nature

*Your Guide to Healing
from the Inside Out*

NANCY ZICK

Acknowledgments

I would like to honor all those who contributed to the completion of this book. It is with deep gratitude and heartfelt thanksgiving that I want to recognize those contributions.

First of all, I give thanks and praise to God, my Creator, for the gifts of listening, healing, and connecting with nature. I am especially thankful that I was chosen to stream these messages and put them in print.

I am grateful to Hay House for offering the "Writer's Workshop" which clearly laid out the process necessary to bring these words into form. I am also grateful to the many authors who have inspired me to heal from the inside out. It is through their listening and writings, that I found the courage to proceed.

I am eternally grateful for my soul sister and guru, Tresa Laferty (teacher for *Wisdom of the Earth Essential Oils*), who opened my eyes and awareness to the wonders of essential oils and taught me how to listen to the plant and tree world. Your guidance and support are appreciated.

I am filled with gratitude for my friend and published author, Barbara Burris, who graciously read through every word, offering amazing insights and helping me stay on track throughout the writing process. Thank you for hanging in there with me and for all of your encouragement.

I am grateful for my friend and published author, Sherry J. Engstrom, for her insightfulness and assistance in overseeing the flow of the finished product. Your support and guidance helped me see each section with new eyes. I truly appreciate your recommendations for bringing the pieces of writings into the whole finished form. Thank you for your gracious support and for encouraging me to grow as a writer.

I offer abundant thanks to all of my soul sisters and beta readers, Barbara and Sherry, Sarah Berg, and Susan Pralle who spent countless hours reading through the finished manuscript before I sent it off to my editor. Your feedback was invaluable and you all helped me blossom in my writing ability. I truly appreciate your support and presence in my life.

I am especially grateful to my editor, Kathleen Henning, who meticulously read through every word and gently guided me to see this work with fresh eyes. Her abundant generosity and support are appreciated beyond words. Thank you for all the love, support, and encouragement you have given to me over the years.

I am thankful for my writing coach, Debby Handrich, for her guidance as I selected a publisher. And I'm grateful for my publisher, BookBaby, who made it possible for me to get this book out into the world.

I am grateful to my husband, Dan, for his patience throughout the process as I spent countless hours secluded in my office writing and rewriting and for respecting my meditation time.

And I would like to close by expressing my gratitude to ALL of my clients, students, retreat participants, and peers who have allowed me to be a small part of their healing journey. My life is blessed by the time we shared. I'm sending much love to all of you.

Table of Contents

Acknowledgments

Introduction   1

Chapter 1: Inspired by Nature   **5**

Essence of Nature in a Bottle   7

Nature = Creation = God   10

Nature Engages the Senses   14

Strength and Endurance Through Tree-hugging   15

Tree-hugging as Our Teacher   16

Messages Through the Essences   17

Meditation: The Enchanted Forest   21

Essential Oil Message Review from Chapter 1: Inspired by Nature   24

Chapter 2: Vibrational Frequencies   **26**

What is Energy?   26

Variations in Vibrational Levels   27

Importance of Raising Our Vibrational Level   28

What Are Chakras?   29

Plant Prana   30

Meditation: A New Perspective   34

Chapter 3: Authenticity   **37**

My Grandma's Garden   37

The Benefits of Weeding   39

Labels   40

Loving Kindness Goes a Long Way   43

Slowing Down   45

Meditation: Becoming Your Authentic Self   48

Essential Oil Message Review from Chapter 3: Authenticity   50

Chapter 4: Mindfulness   **54**

Enjoy Life in This Moment   54

Dreams Awaken Our Senses   58

Integrating Mindfulness   60

Stand Solid Where You Are   62

Meditation: Becoming Mindful   64

Essential Oil Message Review from Chapter 4: Mindfulness   66

Chapter 5: Acceptance   **69**

Judgment: The Opposite of Acceptance   69

Acceptance Moves Us from Exhaustion to Exhilaration   71

Breaking Old Patterns Through Healing the Chakras   72

Meditation: Radiating Love and Acceptance   75

Essential Oil Message Review from Chapter 5: Acceptance   77

Chapter 6: Surrender   **80**

May My Will and Thy Will Be One   80

Leading Without Imposing Your Will   82

Seeing with Jesus' Eyes   84

Meditation: Surrendering Like a River   89

Essential Oil Message Review from Chapter 6: Surrender   91

Chapter 7: Divine Timing   **92**

Manifestation of Visions   92

The Path Unfolds   96

Affirmations Along the Way   97

Meditation: Unlimited Possibilities   100

Essential Oil Message Review from Chapter 7: Divine Timing   102

Chapter 8: Encouragement   **104**

Grandma Nan   104

Stand in Your Truth   107

Courage and Confidence   109

Loneliness Journey   111

Meditation: Releasing Fear   113

Essential Oil Message Review from Chapter 8: Encouragement   115

Chapter 9: Gratitude   **118**

Mindful Gratitude Practice   118

Gratitude Expands the Heart   120

Gratitude: Bringer of Hope   122

Growth Through Gratitude   123

Meditation: A Grateful Heart   127

Essential Oil Message Review from Chapter 9: Gratitude   129

Chapter 10: Joy, Love, and Amazing Grace   **132**

Life Without Joy   132

Nature Expands Joy   135

Through Grace Comes Love   136

Perfectly Imperfect Love   139

Living by Grace, Not Perfection   141

Nature Teaches Unconditional Love   142

Meditation: Healing Grace   145

Essential Oil Message Review from Chapter 10:   147
Joy, Love and Amazing Grace

Chapter 11: Trust   **151**

If You Want to Make God Laugh, Tell Him Your Plans   151

Inner Guidance Positioning System   154

Hold the Vision, Trust the Process   156

Meditation: Trusting in the Flow of Life   159

Essential Oil Message Review from Chapter 11: Trust   161

Chapter 12: Soul Resilience   **162**

Belonging   162

Readjusting Through Energy Shifts   164

Turbulence or Stillness?   165

Your Life Is Sacred   166

Dis-ease of the Spiritual Heart   168

Meditation: Interconnectedness of Life   171

Essential Oil Message Review from Chapter 12: Soul Connection   173

Chapter 13: Truth   **175**

Enough!   175

The Truth of Abundance   177

From Frigid to Amicable   180

Healing from the Inside Out   182

Meditation: Acknowledging Your Truth   185

Essential Oil Message Review from Chapter 13: Truth   187

Appendix: Essential Oil Reference Guide   **189**

Bibliography

Further Reading Suggestions

About the Author

Connections

The warmth of the bright sun shining on my face

Listening to a good book

The smell of freshly tilled soil

Rhythm

Energy from lively music

Kindred spirits

Springtime

Hummingbirds

Walking barefoot in the garden

The wind whispering through the pines

Water roaring down mountain rivers

Taking a swim

To write

To plant

To travel

To sing

To love and be loved.

- 1997

Introduction

"So, in life, some enter the services of fame and others of money, but the best choice is that of these few who spend their time in the contemplation of nature, and as lovers of wisdom."
Pythagoras ("The Father of Philosophy," 570-490 BC)

As far back as my memory allows, I have felt peaceful when in nature. Being outside, meant being inside my sanctuary. I loved sitting on the soft green grassy carpet. I sat for hours searching through the clovers for one with four leaves. I easily became one with the ant as it hauled its load back to the sand hill. Once I even dared to reach out and touch the soft fuzzy bee, OUCH! Unpleasant lesson learned.

I grew up in the city of Kenosha, Wisconsin. I didn't have a forest nearby or even a swimmable lake. My nature escapes were often behind the lilac bush, in the neighbor's willow tree, or on the grass behind the garage. Anywhere hidden from the world. Wherever I was, I imagined what it was like being a bird, a squirrel, or a rabbit: to be free to roam wherever I chose, eat whenever I wanted, play, fly, scurry, or sit and rest in the sun whenever I chose. Their life seemed so simple, natural, and exciting.

At my paternal grandmother's house, I loved being near the flower gardens. The rainbow of colors and fragrances were amazing to me ... petunias, marigolds, roses, white lilies and lily of the valley, and moss roses in pink, magenta, yellow and orange ... so much color and so many shades of green. No wonder my favorite color is green!

We lived near Lake Michigan, which was more like an ocean to me than a lake. It was too cold and too rough to swim, but I enjoyed walking along the gigantic rocks. I watched the waves crashing along the shore and discovered the treasures they left behind: driftwood and polished stones and glass as smooth as velvet. The beach was not made of soft sand but instead it contained trillions of tiny coarse rocks, and it always had an unpleasant odor of dead fish. Often, I came across fish carcasses the seagulls had left behind.

The most exciting nature escapes for me happened when we went camping. I was surrounded by nature day and night. I ventured off, away from our campsite, near enough so I was within earshot of my parents' calls but far enough away to feel as though I was in my own world. There, my imagination soared to great heights as the ferns became my shelter and the canopy of trees became my roof. At night, I lay on the grassy hill and looked at the vast array of twinkling lights, diamonds dazzling in the darkened sky, fascinated by the patterns they created. I was lulled to sleep by the humming of the crickets and beetles and awakened in the morning by the chorus of the cheery birds.

It is my hope and prayer, as you read this book, you will open yourself up to the childlike state of pure existence, unleashing your imagination to take you to the depths of nature, where you, too, will be able to connect more deeply with nature's amazing gifts.

A Tribute to Laurel Leaf

Oh, noble Laurel Leaf, your minty scent brings me back in time
to a beautiful garden with a stone wall.

I'm sure I've been here before, surrounded by your fragrance
and beauty, carefree and full of joy.

You have guided and healed me to come to a place of total trust.

Your gentle strength has pulled out of me that which has served
its purpose and is no longer needed.

Your wisdom has brought opportunities of peace and healing to
those who have needed it.

Your love and protection have brought me courage.

May I forever honor you for the noble presence that you are.

My heart is filled with gratitude for your presence in my life.

Thanks and praise are given to our Creator for bringing us together.

May we be a blessing to all those who choose a healing path.

- 2014

Chapter 1

Inspired by Nature

"Look deep into nature, and then you will understand everything better."Albert Einstein (Einstein, 2020)

My early passion for connecting with nature seemingly faded through my teen and early adult life, although I did choose to move out of the city and into the countryside filled with lakes, trees, and abundant wildlife. The busyness of life took over, and even though I longingly gazed out my window as I was doing dishes, I rarely found time to simply "be" in nature.

Don't get me wrong, I always sought out opportunities to hike, cycle, cross-country ski, camp, canoe, or sit around the campfire. But I was focused more on the respite it brought to me from tending to family, work, or household obligations. I wasn't tuned in to listening at that point in my life…or perhaps I was, but just wasn't aware of it.

I am currently in my sixth decade and I no longer resist the urge to be in nature. Over the past few decades, I began surrounding myself with opportunities to get into the great outdoors. I started gardening and absolutely loved burying my fingers and toes into the fresh soil and tending to the growing plants that nourished my family. I began to appreciate and tend to a bed of perennials that morphed into two beds, then three. I began communing with the weeds, birds, and bees--even the pesky insects who were wanting to share in my abundance.

My desire to garden manifested mostly because my second child was highly allergic to many foods. This blessed gift increased my awareness of how important it was to nourish our bodies with healthily sourced plant-based items. It also led me to search out alternatives to the typical medicinal regime. This brought essential oils into my life. For over twenty years, I have been using nature's essences to support my own and my family's wellness.

In 2011 I received a "knowingness" I was to write a book. The title was given to me: Connecting with Nature. As I sat at my computer, a small portion of this book took form. My skills for listening still needed to be awakened. Therefore, it sat for many years, a work in progress without any progress. I read books on writing, I attended workshops on writing. I dabbled here and there in writing. But the source of writing was missing ... listening to the still, small voice within. Totally unaware, I really was writing, as I journaled on a regular basis; I simply didn't see the connection it had to writing a book.

My life's journey led me into the holistic health field through massage, yoga, and energy healing. I also eventually became a certified medicinal aromatherapist. The practice of meditation became more prevalent in my life. I began hearing messages from the plant world as I worked in my gardens. The first one was loud and clear: "Burdock Root." I had been pulling weeds and came to a very stubborn one. I had no idea what Burdock Root was, but she clearly let me know. After the second or third time of those words repeating themselves in my head, I laughed and decided to go look it up. Sure enough! The weed I was pulling at was Burdock Root. I didn't know whether to leave her alone or continue to pull her out. But I found the challenge amusing!

Essence of Nature in a Bottle

In the summer of 2014, I felt the nudge to take the Level One Medicinal Aromatherapy Certification offered through Wisdom of the Earth, a reputable essential oil company based in Sedona, Arizona. Throughout the twenty-hour intensive weekend, my classmates and I not only learned about 100+ essential oils; we also were given many occasions to hone our intuitive skills and open ourselves up to "listen to" and "be guided by" the various essences. These experiences included meditation, movement therapy, energy healing, and a shamanic journey. We engaged in opportunities to allow our hands (not our eyes) to guide us to the essence to use in each activity. Trusting in my intuition was something I had experienced previously; however, in the past I often interrupted the flow by thinking too much about what I was receiving. In order to receive our completion certificate, we had three months to research one particular essential oil we were drawn to. The research requirement also included not only case studies on our own personal use but also studies of its use with our clients, family, or friends. This weekend served as the turning point for me to open up even more to trusting in Divine inner guidance.

On the Monday after I completed the training, I sat down and made a list of all of the oils I was drawn to throughout the weekend experience. It wasn't feasible for me to purchase all of them, so I trusted I was led to the ones I "needed" the most. Among them, I knew that one would become my research companion. I waited to see which it would be.

The oils arrived on Wednesday and I carefully unwrapped each one and placed them on my home altar, labels facing away from me. Thursday morning, during my prayer/meditation time, I felt called to ceremoniously choose my oil. I closed my eyes, set the intention that I would be guided, and decided to hold my hands above the oils to feel their energy. I knew one would eventually feel stronger than the others, or so I thought. With my eyes still closed, as I was hovering over, the middle finger on my left hand dropped down and lightly touched the lid of one of the bottles. I thought, *"Oops, my hands are too close"* and immediately lifted my hands a bit higher. Once again, instantly my middle left finger dropped down and touched a lid. I was moving towards being annoyed with myself when it clicked *"That's my oil!!!"* I picked her up, held her close to my heart thanking her and then looked at the label. It was Laurel Leaf! I was thrilled that she chose me to experience her energy.

She immediately went to work. I sat with her once I opened the bottle and allowed her delicious fragrance to waft through my nostrils. I allowed her to guide me as to how I was to use her. *"Top of the head"* she said. So, I obliged. Then she said, *"And the bottom of your feet"*. I followed her instruction. I instantly felt her energy in my feet. After basking in this awhile, I set her down next to me. I was instantly in love. I began my usual prayer time which included praying for my clients scheduled for that day. I was aware of Laurel Leaf's presence and she said, *"I need to go with you today…"* I smiled and started to put her in my purse when she continued, *"and you will use me with your first client."* That piqued my curiosity! I decided to read her label and saw that one of her abilities is to work with Lyme disease. My jaw dropped. My first client was undergoing treatment for chronic Lyme and had been dealing with the many side effects of the treatment protocol. This affirmation gave me such a strong feeling of TRUST at being guided.

When I met with my client, I shared with her my experience of the morning. She was open and willing to trust me, so I let Laurel Leaf guide me. *"On her neck in the back at the base of the skull."* I obediently listened. This was a massage client, but I felt a strong urge to include energy work too. Later in the massage, Laurel Leaf called me to use her on my clients' feet. I listened, all the while feeling a connection to the guidance. Afterwards, my client stated she really felt different about the massage. She said she felt more energy and she had gone deeper into her session. Thank you, Laurel Leaf!

I continue to embrace Laurel Leaf's lovely fragrance on a regular basis and believe by utilizing her, she has helped to clear any energetic blocks I had to embracing my inner guidance. As noted in the Appendix, one of her amazing qualities is a bringer of courage. Indeed, she has opened that for me. This guidance is available to everyone. Many times, throughout my life, I have doubted my intuition. With practice and intention, it is available. If you have the desire to listen to your intuition, a God-given gift we all have, allow nature to be your companion to assist you on your journey. If circumstances prevent you from experiencing the natural world, turn to nature in a bottle, the amazing gift of essential oils.

This experience opened my awareness to listening to the essences as they called. Sometimes it was for me personally. Other times it was for a client I was serving. Eventually I was led to use them in my meditation practice and the messages began to flow. It was over a year later when I clearly heard the inner voice within say that I had all I needed to complete this book. I still didn't quite understand until one day I was told "Re-read your journals. It is all there." Here is an excerpt from my journal at a time when I used the essential oil of Ravintsara during my meditation practice:

All of nature is excited to be with you at this time in your life. Especially as you are becoming more and more connected to the plants and trees. Trust that through nature you are guided and will be given the words you need to say. Know that you will be touching more lives than you can imagine and what is spoken is exactly what needs to be heard. Release worries about convincing certain people as they are on their own path, which may be different than yours. Release them with love. You are not about competition. You are about sharing the love of the plant and tree kingdom with others. Keep that focus at all times. You will be guided with each step, including all of the details that are floating through your mind. You are loved and supported in all aspects of your life.

I offer with joy and enthusiasm the gift which was bestowed to me. In the following chapters, I have categorized the messages under themes that go along with the message I received. I have also indicated the essential oil I used and included a brief summary of each essential oil's healing properties in the Appendix. It is my sincere prayer and wish that you, too, will find inspiration from these messages. But before we delve into the message portion, let me set the stage for you.

Nature = Creation = God

"You didn't come into this world. You came out of it, like a wave from the ocean." Alan W. Watts (Watts, 1974)

To me, Nature equals God. Nature is where I experience total communion with God and the beautiful world He/She has created. I'm reminded of this through a song I used to sing with the children at my church: "All God's Critters Got a Place in the Choir." In this simple song, we're reminded that every part of creation has its place and is to be honored and recognized. This sounds so logical, but how easy is it to apply it throughout our daily lives? If we truly believed we all have a place, then discrimination would be non-existent, wars over boundaries would be non-existent, poverty would be non-existent, and governments would cooperate and collaborate on environmental concerns and issues of human rights and dignity.

We each came here in our own unique form. Each with a gift to offer to the world. What has caused us to be so divided? As I pondered these deep questions, I used Marjoram to connect me to the Divine message:

> *Imagine what it is like to be a seed starting from the moment the soil engulfs you and begins to warm you until you burst from the earth to start your cycle of growth. Can you feel the excitement as you entered this world? Look around you and be aware of all of your friends surrounding you. Enjoy the vibrational energy of excitement as you feel their love and they feel your love. Notice the other beings that delight in your presence--butterflies, bees, ants, beetles, worms, birds--and feel a connection to all. Bask in the joy of this moment.*

> *God wants all beings to feel this connectedness, this sense of communion, knowing that all existence is present to support one another unconditionally. Even those who have caused devastation. They, too, have served their purpose. They are here to teach resilience and perseverance. They help you grow stronger so you can honor your purpose. All are here*

to support one another. God's desire is communion with all beings. You are here to be an example of this.

The time is NOW for all of us to feel this connectedness. We need to come together as ONE to heal and repair the damage that has already been done to Mother Earth and her inhabitants. We have been given an opportunity to slow down, honor, enjoy, and revere nature, and arise with a whole new perspective on how our daily choices are hurting our planet and one another. We can clearly see what needs to be done to engage in a global effort of healing. As I am writing this, the world is in the middle of the Novel Coronavirus, COVID-19, pandemic. When blue skies are currently (spring 2020) present in Los Angeles, that speaks volumes. I'm grateful I am living through this transformative experience. Each day of this global pandemic, I humbly look at what changes I can make. I see the shifts in the Earth's atmosphere due to less mobilization. I see the shifts in the lives around me as they engage as families and couples instead of going their separate ways. I see people reaching out to help other people. What can I do differently in my life?

How about you? Are you feeling the pulse of change knocking at your door?

What amazing innovations are you inspired to bring forth to restore and preserve our planet?

Perhaps you, too, can find simple ways to make changes which will affect the greater whole in the long run. How can you get this message out to the people in your circle? One step at a time, we can make this happen! Below are some simple suggestions:

Shop less often

    ❧ Plan meals ahead

- Make a concise list
- Buy in bulk whenever possible
- Collaborate with neighbors for small grocery runs

Reduce Commuting

- Whenever possible, save energy by working from home
- Initiate a plan in your workplace that supports conserving energy
- If you can't work from home, carpool to reduce car emissions
- Suggest shorter work weeks (i.e. work 4 10's instead of 5 8's)

Planting

- Growing your own vegetables, greens and herbs can be very rewarding
- Trees help clean the air and you are giving back to the Earth
- House plants help purify the indoor air
- Flowers not only beautify our Mother Earth but can also be functional depending on species

Earth Day every day

- Recycle whenever possible and reduce waste as much as possible
- Start a compost pile or bin
- Make it a point to pick up garbage when you see it, rather than frown at it

Nature Engages the Senses

As I chose to become more connected to nature, I found my senses were heightened. Colors were more vibrant, sounds more acute, fragrances blended and caught my attention, and I became aware of the gentle brush of wind on my skin. But a new way of using my senses seemed to be awakened from within. I appreciated Mother Earth's gifts. I reconnected with my desire to be more contemplative. As I closed my eyes while meditating, I was able to see by listening. The gentle flutter of wings gave me a clear vision of the bird landing nearby, even though I wasn't using my physical eyes to see her. I heard the bird's song simply by gazing into the bird's eyes, even if I was listening to meditative music with earbuds.

The practice of tuning into nature and connecting on a deeper level is available to everyone. So many people are drawn to nature, as I was, but in the process, they fail to tune into the messages available to them. Either they are talking with one another or they're engaging in activities that distract them from truly connecting. It seems to me this is clearly part of the demise of human nature. In America especially, we have allowed ourselves to become distracted from the gift of nature from which we all came. And worse yet, we have become complacent about giving back to and respecting nature. Going back to the message that came through Marjoram:

God wants all beings to feel this connectedness, this sense of communion, knowing that all existence is present to support one another unconditionally. Even those who have caused devastation. They, too, have served their purpose. They are here to teach resilience and perseverance. They help you grow stronger so you can honor your purpose. All are here to support one another. God's desire is communion with all beings. You are here to be an example of this.

I challenge you, the reader, to step out in nature each and every day, even if you live in the city. Find a bush or a planter of flowers or a water fountain or a tree and pause for a moment. Allow your thoughts to be still for this moment and tune in to what you see, hear, smell, or feel. Can you find beauty and diversity in the bark of the tree? Do you notice the buds that haven't yet opened on plants? Do the leaves look vibrant and full of life or do they look sad and in need of tender loving care? What does the sound of water bring to mind? What do you hear in the bird's melodies? What emotions does the wind invoke?

Can you sense a simple message nature's bringing you?

Strength and Endurance Through Tree-hugging

And now you are likely wondering, is she a tree hugger? Truth be told, yes, I am. And I love every minute of it. The energy exchange between the tree and me is unexplainable. Try it! There is an unconditional love exchange which is difficult to put into words. I've even communed with the small trees planted around Ground Zero in New York City. They have a lot to say and can bring humanity hope in a seemingly hopeless world.

While visiting the 911 Memorial Park, I was taking in the elements as my sons and I quietly absorbed our surroundings. There was a feeling of reverence and sorrow for the tragedy and loss of lives, human and otherwise. Whomever designed this beautiful memorial must have researched the meaning of the elements. The sound of the continuous flow of water in the manmade infinity waterfalls reminded me of the flow of life: falling and rising, life-giving, gentle but powerful. I felt a gentle breeze carrying the heavy, ominous spirit away and filling the space with a reverent holiness. I reflected on all of the lives lost, not only those who worked in the Twin Towers but also the lives of the emergency crews, and people who were in the surrounding area gripped with fear. A gentle feeling of hope was now emerging through this beautiful memorial. I noticed the stately beauty of the 400 trees surrounding the pools. I paused for a moment and asked one of the trees what she represented. As my hands took in her pulse, I clearly heard, *"strength and endurance."* I thanked her and honored her for sharing. A volunteer later told us the trees were not native to New York, but were Swamp Oaks brought in from Virginia. When I looked up the metaphysical meaning of "oak," I read "endurance, strength, longevity." This confirmed exactly what I had heard.

Onsite, there was one other significant tree. This radiant Pear Tree was surrounded by a fence. She had been retrieved a month after 911 by rescue workers. She was buried in the rubble and debris. At one time, she had stood outside of the North Tower. The rescue workers saw signs of life and removed her. She was relocated to her temporary home in another park in NYC. Ten years later, she was brought back and affectionately named the Survivor Tree. She stands as a reminder of the resilience and perseverance of all survivors.

Tree-hugging as Our Teacher

"Study nature, love nature, stay close to nature.
It will never fail you." Frank Lloyd Wright (Wright, 2020)

There is a lot to learn from the natural world when we tune in to listen. Trees have an intricate communication system, using their roots to "speak" to one another. They have a living network hidden beneath the surface, constantly sending messages about impending diseases, pests, or droughts. Through their unique internet connection, they support one another mostly without human intervention. If this piques your interest, I suggest reading The Hidden Life of Trees by Peter Wohlleben (Wohlleben, 2016) . Mr. Wohlleben spent over 20 years working for the forestry commission in Germany. His book takes you on an enticing journey deep into the forest to uncover the fascinating and thought-provoking hidden life of trees. The following story of my beloved maple tree powerfully illustrates the connection between man and nature.

At one time, I had a gorgeous maple tree outside of my office window. She was big and old. She provided the most splendid shade on a hot summer's day before my office was air conditioned. Her trunk was approximately three feet in diameter indicating she was quite old. One summer, she was struck by lightning and split in two right down her middle, almost to the ground but not quite. I was devastated. The local tree "doctors" came and drilled a bolt through her middle, drawing the two sides together. A nut was put in place and ropes temporarily secured her while she healed her wound. The amazing thing is she not only survived, she thrived! After several years had passed, she had covered over her saving bolt with fresh bark and any newcomer would never have known she had been damaged. In this case, she needed human intervention to help her heal and restore. She provided life to animals, birds, and insects, and she shared her shade and beauty. Human ingenuity and technology saved her. It is a powerful reminder to engage our senses and understand the elements as we commune with nature. This will surely open our heart connection.

Messages Through the Essences

Recently, I was reminded of my call to write and experience the essences for myself on a more personal level. I received the message telling me profound insights will be revealed through them and I am to trust and believe.

It is important for you to start today and continue to listen daily. Remember to include the essences with clients, friends, family and especially yourself as they will be your catalyst to gratitude, love, joy, peace and hope. This will bring you into the upward spiral your soul desires.

I believe we are all extensions of our Divine Creator. For me, listening to nature is listening to God (or the Universe, or Divine Intelligence, or Source…whichever term you are comfortable using). It isn't an audible voice speaking. It is an inner knowing. Before starting my meditation time, I listen to which essence is calling to me. I sit with it for a moment allowing it to guide me as to how I am to use it. Most often I am called to place it on one chakra *(see detailed description of chakras in next chapter)* or another, but sometimes I am beckoned to simply inhale her beautiful gift. I then go into a meditative state and allow whatever comes to the surface to flow. Once the message stream stops, I pick up my pen and journal what I hear. Many times, the messages are speaking to me about a particular situation but, as I later reflected on these messages, it became clear to me the messages weren't just for me. I am repeating here, the clear message from Marjoram:

God wants all beings to feel this connectedness, this sense of communion, knowing that all existence is present to support one another unconditionally. Even those who have caused devastation. They, too, have served their purpose. They are here to teach resilience and perseverance. They help you grow stronger so you can honor your purpose. All are here to support one another. God's desire is communion with all beings. You are here to be an example of this.

It is through the passion of wanting to share what I have learned along my soul's journey, what I have found to be true within me, that I am sharing with you. Each of us is on our own journey and we need to honor and respect that of ourselves. I bring these messages to you with unconditional love in my heart for each one of you, whether we agree or not, with no judgment. My hope is that through the stories I share of my personal journey, that you, too, will find connection and inspiration to use nature as the key to unlock the door of your healing journey. We are here as one collective presence on this planet we call Earth. Feel the support and unconditional love present for each of us. Be inspired by nature to find your path. It is there, waiting for you.

In the pages to follow, each chapter contains anecdotes of my experiences followed by the essential oil I was led to use relating to the theme. I also share the message I received and thought-provoking questions to help take readers further into their own inquiry. At the end of each chapter, you will find a guided meditation and a review of the messages referenced in that chapter. I encourage you to utilize the list of essential oils in the Appendix to further your knowledge of essential oils. Included in the descriptions, you will find suggestions on how to use their healing properties to support your emotional/mental/spiritual well-being.

I encourage you, whenever possible, to use the essence listed in the pages to follow, allowing her energy to merge with yours. Or use an essential oil you have on hand. Give yourself a moment to slowly take three deep breaths, as you inhale this beautiful gift of nature. If you are called to do so, you may apply this essence to one or more of your chakras, being mindful of essences which may be "hot" on tender skin (see Appendix for guidance). Alternately, you may choose to diffuse the oil while meditating with her. Whichever you choose, use this practice as a mindfulness moment to connect you, through nature, to your true inner spirit. Relax … Enjoy … Heal!

Meditation

The Enchanted Forest

Begin by finding a comfortable place to sit or lie down. With your eyes closed or with a softened gaze, begin to focus on your breath … release any lingering thoughts and fears.

Focusing on the in breath and out breath, the mind and body become still and relaxed.

When you are fully present, imagine you are walking along a path through a meadow. The sun is shining down on you and you can feel the cool crisp breeze blowing on your face. Notice the tall grasses waving a warm welcome to you.

As you look ahead, you see an enticing, lush forest. Your pace quickens as the tree kingdom beckons you to be embraced by its presence.

Approaching the tree line, you begin to hear the wind rustling the leaves … it is a sound like water rushing down a mountain stream. Occasionally you are startled by a leaf falling off of a tree as it lands in your hair. You continue strolling through this serene woodland.

Pause and breathe deeply. Smell the damp brown leaves and woody scent of autumn, reminding you of days gone by when you'd rake a pile of leaves and jump into them. This brings a smile to your face.

Continuing along the path in the forest, you are aware that the birds are your constant companions. Even though you rarely can see them, you listen to their chattering to one another as they prepare for the winter cold.

Your attention is brought to a distinctive goose call and the responding calls from the rest of the flock. Their calls can be heard for quite a distance. One flock passes above you and you watch as they stay in their V formation. They are so high they look like flying ants!

The bees seem to take no heed of your presence. Their soft buzzing sound is heard periodically throughout your journey. You have a deep respect for their presence, even though you may not enjoy their company much, you observe how they are working at gathering nectar in winter preparation. You are amazed at how diligently they work, going from flower to flower, all day long.

You realize you are approaching your favorite spot of the forest, the Enchanted Forest. You hasten your pace.

Reaching the tall pines, you automatically breathe deeply, this time to smell the minty-fresh fragrance of the pine. The dried needles crunch as you search for the perfect place to rest.

Finding the perfect spot deep within the walls of the pine, where a glimmer of sunlight is shining through from above, you nestle yourself comfortably at the base of a tree. As you tilt your face upward to catch the warm rays of the sun, you close your eyes absorbing the sweet sounds and aromas.

The first sound you are aware of is the whispering of the wind through the pine. It is like a gentle lullaby, soothing to the soul. The occasional rustling of a chipmunk or squirrel snaps your attention back, but only briefly.

The tall trees surround you like protective guards and you feel safe and removed from the world of turmoil, connecting to the peace and harmony within, with unabandoned freedom.

Linger here as long as necessary, embracing the harmony of nature. When you are ready, carefully retrace your steps back to the well-worn path. As your journey nears the end, you look back and see the tops of your guards waving good-bye.

Slowly bring yourself back to the space you are occupying. Begin to wiggle your toes and fingers ... bring your awareness back to your breath, you are feeling comforted and peaceful as this connection with nature settles into your being.

When you are ready, open your eyes, and move into your day with a smile.

Essential Oil Message
Review from Chapter 1

Inspired by Nature

Ravintsara

All of nature is excited to be with you at this time in your life. Especially as you are becoming more and more connected to the plants and trees. Trust that through nature you are guided and will be given the words you need to say. Know that you will be touching more lives than you can imagine and what is spoken is exactly what needs to be heard. Release worries about convincing certain people as they are on their own path, which may be different than yours. Release them with love. You are not about competition. You are about sharing the love of the plant and tree kingdom with others. Keep that focus at all times. You will be guided with each step, including all of the details that are floating through your mind. You are loved and supported in all aspects of your life.

Marjoram

Imagine what it is like to be a seed starting from the moment the soil engulfs you and begins to warm you until you burst from the earth to start your cycle of growth. Can you feel the excitement as you entered this world? Look around you and be aware of all of your friends surrounding you. Enjoy the vibrational energy of excitement as you feel their love and they feel your love. Notice the other beings that delight in your presence--butterflies, bees, ants, beetles, worms, birds--and feel a connection to all. Bask in the joy of this moment.

God wants all beings to feel this connectedness, this sense of communion, knowing that all existence is present to support one another unconditionally. Even those who have caused devastation. They, too, have served their purpose. They are here to teach resilience and perseverance. They help you grow stronger so you can honor your purpose. All are here to support one another. God's desire is communion with all beings. You are here to be an example of this.

Chapter 2

Vibrational Frequencies

Everything is energy and that's all there is to it.

What is Energy?

The above quote, often erroneously attributed to Albert Einstein, sums up the definition of energy. Energy is the invisible force that animates life. There are many different types of energy. For the purpose of this book, energy will be used to describe your personal vibrational frequency. This energy frequency is a culmination of every thought, feeling, and action from every lifetime you have lived. It surrounds and permeates all cells in your body. It is your Divine signature, the essence of your soul. Each of our vibrational frequencies is a direct reflection of our thoughts, feelings, beliefs, word choices and how we move through the world as we take care of ourselves, the Earth, and all her occupants.

Variations in Vibrational Levels

Higher vibration equals more light. More light means the light particles vibrate faster. When light particles vibrate faster, you will experience higher consciousness and a stronger connection to your soul and God-self. Love is your source of direction. Higher vibrations are the gateway to love, joy, peace, hope, gratitude, recognizing divinity in oneself and in others, and feeling aligned with your soul. You move through life with grace and ease.

Lower vibration means the opposite is true. Lower vibration equals slower or less light. Less light means the light particles vibrate slower and become more condensed. Your energy then feels heavy and you don't feel aligned with your soul and your Divine self. You operate from a fear-based perspective. Lower vibrations carry the heaviness of shame, guilt, fear, blame, judgment, resentment, anger, jealousy, unforgiveness, addiction, conditional love, lack of self-worth, greed, and the feeling of separation. This often brings poor health and feelings of lethargy.

In her book Raise Your Vibration, Sabrina Reber states: *"Our physical bodies, those parts of us that are not eternal, are interpenetrated and surrounded by our eternal divine essence, consisting of our emotional, mental and spiritual energetic layers."* (Reber, 2013) This makes us multi-dimensional, energetic spiritual beings living a human experience in physical form. As French philosopher Pierre Teilhard de Chardin so eloquently put it: *"We are not human beings having a spiritual experience. We are spiritual beings having a human experience."* (Chardin, 2020)

Importance of Raising Our Vibrational Level

Self-empowerment comes when we are aware of and align with the energies of our emotional, mental and spiritual states of being. This allows our soul to integrate all of our layers and will bring us to a place of wholeness and connectedness with our Higher Power, the Universe, God, or whatever name you give the Creator of all life. This takes concerted effort and awareness of the imbalances that present themselves. Throughout our lives, opportunities arise for us to engage in a spiritual detox. The Light shines on our darkness and it is up to us to rise up, heal, transmute, and release our individual darkness. Some refer to this darkness as our shadow side or the shadow within.

For me, this is an ongoing process. I recognize the process when it arises and I have enough tools in place to work my way through the layers. In this book, I have attempted to share with you my personal healing journey and some of those tools. It is my prayer that these suggestions will help you as well. As author, intuitive and spiritual teacher, Cynthia Olivera shared recently: *"Universal peace and brotherhood/sisterhood will reign on this planet. We are being shown our shadow side in order to love, forgive and raise our frequencies. Keep the balance, stay in your heart, and help others."* We are witnessing our capacity to be part of a larger reality, a more inclusive universal and multidimensional community that comes after we make our way through this tunnel of darkness. As we face and address our own shadow side, our hearts become more open to help and serve others. We simply need to live our lives at a higher vibrational level, benefitting not only ourselves, but all other beings in our lives.

According to modern-day mystics, in 2012 we entered into a historic time when the universe is shifting. We are moving out of the Industrial Age which fostered in a hunger for power, greed, and a host of other lower vibrational energies. Currently, we are in the Golden Age of planetary ascension and anyone choosing to be on this planet will experience the chaos of the world. As Reber states, *"The chaos of the world is a reflection of our own inner chaos. It is not that we have more darkness on the planet; it is that we have more light permeating the planet, forcing the darkness within each of us to rise to the surface to be healed, transmuted, and released."* (Reber p.7, emphasis added)

Clearly, now is the time to do our internal work of processing the lower vibrations. The first step is awareness. Having the desire to release and heal the energies that no longer serve a purpose in our life is the opening of awareness. The next step is becoming aware of our chakras, our individual energy centers, and purposefully bringing them into balance.

What Are Chakras?

Our energetic body, also known as the subtle body, surrounds and passes through our physical body. There are tens of thousands of energy lines that extend out around each of us, a full arm's length in all directions. These energy lines are horizontal, vertical, transverse, and spiral in nature. Our chakras are energy vortices formed by the interception of these energy lines, creating a spiral. Chakra is a Sanskrit word which means "wheel of light". Sanskrit is an ancient spiritual language used across many Eastern cultures to this day. Our chakras regulate the spiritual life-force energy, also known as prana or chi. If our chakras are not functioning properly, our health becomes vulnerable. The chakras are found starting at the base of the spine and extend upwards to the top of the head. The first three chakras correlate with the three-dimensional world we live in, earth/matter/physicality. The top three chakras lead us into a state of heightened spiritual development, heaven/spirit/intuition. The middle chakra, the Heart Chakra, is midway between the upper and lower chakras. The Heart Chakra serves to balance the lower chakras, which helps us stay grounded on Earth and is the gateway to the upper chakras. The upper chakras allow us to draw in an expanded amount of Divine love, wisdom and healing energies.

These seven main chakras send out energies affecting people and events around us. If a chakra is blocked or distorted, the intake of energy will be depleted or excessive. This, in turn, affects not only us, but also people with whom we interact. Throughout this book, when referenced, I am referring to these seven main energy centers or chakras.

Aromatherapy is one method of balancing the chakras. Plants and trees also have an energy life force in and around them, each vibrating at its own unique frequency. This energy is referred to as plant prana. Utilizing the essence of the plant through the use of aromatherapy provides us with the opportunity to tap into its frequency to help balance ours. A substance with a higher vibrational frequency can raise a lower frequency due to the principle of entrainment. Entrainment is the tendency for two oscillating bodies to lock together so they vibrate in harmony. This helps us understand the effect plant prana can have on our personal electromagnetic frequency.

Plant Prana

Pure plant prana, also referred to as chi, universal life-force energy, has the highest frequencies of any measured natural substance. Remembering back to our early years of science, we recall the basics of vibration, that every atom in the universe has a specific vibratory or periodic motion and each motion has a frequency (defined as the number of oscillations per second) measured in Hertz. The vibrational frequency of therapeutic herbs and plants reflects the integrity of the elements and enzymes embodied within its substance—it's bio-energy or life force and its original intent.

In the early 1990's, Bruce Tainio of Tainio Technology & Technique, Inc., built the first frequency monitor in the world called Tainio Technology Frequency Monitoring Device. This device was a calibrated frequency monitor used to measure the bio-electrical frequencies of plant nutrients, herbs and plant life, and foods. Although this device is no longer available, the findings from using this device were quite interesting. Here is a list of average frequencies of a sampling of plant prana that were measured:

- Rose (Rosa damascene) 320 MHz
- Lavender (Lavendula angustifolis) 118 MHz
- Myrrh (Commiphora myrrha) 105 MHz
- Blue Chamomile (Matricaria recutita) 105 MHz
- Juniper (Juniperus osteosperma) 98 MHz
- Aloes/Sandalwood (Santalum album) 96 MHz
- Angelica (Angelica archangelica) 85 MHz
- Peppermint (Mentha peperita) 78 MHz
- Galbanum (Ferula gummosa) 56 MHz
- Basil (Ocimum basilicum) 52 MHz

When we compare them to the following list, we see that most of the plant prana frequencies measured higher than the human body:

- Brain frequency range 72-90 MHz
- Normal brain frequency 72 MHz and Genius brain frequency 80-82 MHz
- Human body 62-78 MHz

✒ Thyroid and Parathyroid gland 62-68 MHz

✒ Thymus gland 65-68 MHz

✒ Heart 67-70 MHz

✒ Liver 55-60 MHz

✒ Lungs 58-65 MHz

✒ Pancreas 60-80 MHz

Tainio also found that the plant prana frequencies of vegetables and herbs can be higher if grown organically and eaten fresh-picked:

✒ Fresh foods & herbs 20-27 Hz

✒ Dried foods & herbs 15-22 Hz

✒ Processed/Canned Food 0 Hz

Tainio and his colleagues determined that when a person's frequency drops below the optimum healthy range, the immune system is compromised. Human cells can start to change (mutate) when their frequency drops below 62 MHz. Below is a glimpse at some of the findings:

✒ Colds and flu start at 57-60 MHz

✒ Disease starts at 58 MHz

✒ Candida overgrowth starts at 55 MHz

✒ Receptive to Epstein Barr at 52 MHz

✒ Receptive to Cancer at 42 MHz

✒ Death process begins at 20 MHz

We can use this information to help us understand the importance of energy and the effect energy depletion has on our bodies. Factors outside of the body also affect our vibrational frequency.

Pathogens, pollutants, and processed/canned foods can diminish a person's frequency. Even thoughts and feelings have a vibratory quality that forms a measurable frequency. It has been shown that a negative mental state can lower a person's frequency by 10-12 MHz. Likewise, we can raise our frequencies through positive thoughts and emotions and by using high vibrational frequency devices, such as a BioMat, Crystal, or Sound Therapies. Positive mental attitude, prayer, or meditation can raise human vibrations by 10-15 MHz. (Aetherna, 2018) (Chanel, 2013)

Many scientists and researchers continue to study vibrational frequencies. Our planet is constantly in motion and recent studies have shown these frequencies vary, dependent on many factors. It is my hope that by providing you with a glimpse into the science of vibrations, you will have a better understanding of the importance of doing our individual and collective shadow work: that is to heal, transmute and release our individual darkness. Throughout the following chapters, I courageously share the experiences I have had with facing my shadow side and the methods I implemented to raise my vibrational level.

"The art of healing comes from nature and not from the physician. Therefore, the physician must start from nature with an open mind." Paracelsus (Paracelsus, 2020)

Meditation

A New Perspective

Begin by settling in as you find a comfortable position. Close your eyes or have a soft gaze on a non-movable object.

Begin to follow the rhythm of your breath, allowing thoughts to drift through, releasing attachment to thoughts and concerns.

Slowly inhaling … counting 1 – 2 – 3 – 4

Exhaling even more slowly, begin to scan your body for any places in need of relaxing.

Using your breath as you relax your forehead … your jaw … your shoulders … your arms … feel the heaviness of your hands … your fingers.

Continue to release each part of your body until you no longer sense any tension.

Using your mind's eye, observe yourself sitting where you are … as if you are floating above, gazing down.

Take in the entire room from a bird's-eye perspective.

Allow yourself to move further and further away … through the ceiling … above the roof.

Gazing down, notice the building or space all around you.

Continuing to float upwards … take in the whole city or countryside around you...

Seeing your country and the surrounding countries.

Allow yourself to ascend further and further into space ... As you do, look around you, observing the universe encompassing you as you are floating.

Notice the peacefulness, quietness unlike anything you've experienced ... notice the stars ... the planets ... the vastness of the universe.

Searching, you observe our planet ... how peaceful it looks ... become aware of the deep blues of the oceans ... the richness of the land formations ... the cotton-like clouds hovering around it.

Take it all in ... realize you, too, are a part of this beautiful place ... you, too, can contribute to the good of the planet ... your mere existence is vital to the health and well-being of all.

Stay in this space as long as you need to ... allow it to wash over you ... allow it to bring you a fresh, new perspective of the interconnectedness of all.

Slowly, begin to descend to earth. Floating gently as your country is coming into view ... notice the area you are currently in.

Find yourself floating in the room or space above you.

Take in how peaceful you look ... completing the descent into your physical form once again, begin to wiggle your fingers ... your toes.

Focus on your breath, feel the rise and fall of the abdomen and chest with every inhale and exhale.

Take a few moments to ponder how significant you really are. You feel empowered to make a difference in your lifetime. Know this sense of peace is within you at all times ... simply tap into it at any moment.

When you are ready ... slowly open your eyes. See life from a new perspective.

A Poem from Rosemary

You are soft and beautiful,

Gentle and strong.

You are bold and subtle

Deep and a song.

You float through the air

Wafting your scent.

Yet you linger and praise

While you make your descent.

What fond memories you bring

Of times gone by.

I enjoy the recall …

My how time seems to fly!

And so, my dear friend

My message today:

"Live each moment to the fullest

As you go along your way."

- 2017

Chapter 3

Authenticity

"One touch of nature makes the whole world kin."
William Shakespeare (Shakespeare, 2020)

My Grandma's Garden

I loved going to visit my grandma's house, a weekly routine for my brother and me when we were growing up. Every Friday after school, my dad packed us up in the car and dropped us off. I delighted in hearing Grandma's stories about life on the farm and I cherished being surrounded by her garden varieties. Her gardens reminded me of the brilliant colors of a kaleidoscope. I would hunt through the grass in her backyard for hours searching for a four-leaf clover, taking in the lovely scents around me.

One day recently, as I prepared for my meditation, I was drawn to Rosemary. Rosemary loves to bring beautiful memories to the surface.

I sat pondering the fond memories of my Grandma's garden and the joy it brought me. After deeply inhaling Rosemary's fresh minty scent, I applied a few drops to the top of my head, the Crown Chakra. The message I received was clear:

You are as unique and beautiful as the vibrant patterns in a kaleidoscope. As you breathe in, each of your cells shifts and changes, and as you exhale, they change again. Through the eyes of nature, all of creation is seen in this beautiful way. As with a kaleidoscope, when the light is obstructed or fades, the vibrancy dims. The colors and shapes are still there but are not as prevalent. This is true with humans as well. Sometimes you encounter circumstances that may dim or shadow your vibrancy. It is still there. It just needs a little light to shine through and bring it back to its full glory. Remember this when you encounter people who are struggling. Shine some light on their kaleidoscopes so they can see their vibrancy once again. Using Rosemary helps you remember the Divine, beautiful, colorful kaleidoscope you are! Peace be with you!

Each one of us is unique and beautiful in our own way. I have gone through phases of my life when my vibrancy was dimmed by circumstances either through unhealthy patterns I had latched onto or from circumstances beyond my control. Struggles are part of life. This reminds me of a passage from the New Testament in the Bible: *"... suffering produces endurance, and endurance produces character and character produces hope, and hope does not disappoint us, because God's love has been poured into our hearts...." Romans 5:3-5 (NRSV)*

Now I can see how much I've grown through challenges. Through each struggle, my spiritual backbone has become stronger.

To live from my authenticity, means I must tune into what is genuine and resonates with what I believe to be true.

It is my hope and prayer that you, too, will find the space to grow from your struggles. Lean on the memories that bring joy and love into your awareness. Lean on the memories that represent the kaleidoscope of your life. And then shine a little light on them to bring you back to your full glory.

The Benefits of Weeding

I find the chore of weeding to be a meditative practice. The resilience of weeds always amazes me. I visualize their roots becoming untangled and freeing up the roots of the plants I intended to be in that particular area. It doesn't seem to bother them (the weeds) at all. Within a few days, week if I'm lucky, they begin to peek their heads out above the ground once again, as if to say, "You can't stop me!" Sometimes, they are so deeply rooted I end up hurting myself in the process of trying to remove them, which was the case with the Burdock Root I spoke about in the introduction. Pull and tug as I did, she not only resisted being removed but she also kept insisting I wake up to who she was, "Burdock Root". When I continued to pull, she persisted, "Burdock Root." It wasn't until she put it on repeat, "Burdock Root, Burdock Root, Burdock Root!" that she actually caught my attention. Humored and needing a reprieve from my back-breaking work, I decided to go look up Burdock Root, as I had no idea what it was. To my surprise, *voila!* there she was. At that point, I had to decide--do I allow her to have her space in my garden or do I remove her? I made the difficult decision to continue to remove her, due to her invasive nature, even though she brought me the amazing gift of awareness.

I share this experience with you as a reminder of all of the people, situations and things in your life that may need to be weeded out. Perhaps you are facing this right now. What "weed" prevents you from being the authentic person you desire to be? The decision has to come from a place of deep discernment. Is this "weed" beneficial to you and your future? How deeply rooted is it? Is it shouting to you in some subconscious way announcing why it is there? Would you grow exponentially, beyond your greatest imaginings, if you removed it? The pungent scent of Sage True brought forth a clear message as I meditated on this:

> *I am here to support you and to take you deeper into your understanding. Stay focused on sharing your Truth. You have been, are, and will be touching many lives. Everyone who hears you is taking in the seeds you are planting. Some will grow slower than others. Keep planting! You have been plucking out the weeds that were stunting your growth. Do not ruminate over them. Let them go. Thank them for the part they played in your life and then release them.*

Perhaps there are seeds you have been planting as well and it is time for you to begin the process of weeding out that which doesn't serve your highest good any more. We all need the "weeds" in our life to bring us the nutrients they have to offer. But there comes a time when they begin to choke out the seeds we are planting. Be mindful of those who are stunting your growth and mindfully release them!

Labels

At times, I find labels useful, and other times I am annoyed with them. For instance, years ago when I was the director of a preschool, I was contacted by the local school Multidisciplinary Team about an incoming student who needed special services. As useful as it was to be working with a team, I found some of our staff had difficulty trying to identify the child first as a child instead of as a "Special Needs" child. Our motto was 'Sharing a Little of God's Love' and we each believed it with all our heart. We believed we were in each child's life to share God's love with them. It challenged us to work outside of the label and trust there was a plan bigger than we could see.

Religious labels are another example of labels that can be good or get annoying. For instance, I was born and raised in the Christian tradition. I embraced the teachings and lived my life to the best of my ability by the principles of Christianity. Over the past couple of decades, I have found it increasingly difficult to identify with that particular label. I continue to follow Christ's teachings, but the label of Christianity carries with it a vast array of beliefs from conservative to liberal, such that I'm not comfortable associating with that label any more.

Throughout these years of discovering and owning my authenticity, I have left behind many labels that once formed my identity. In 2015 and again in 2018, I attended the Parliament of the World's Religions gathering. This conference consists of thousands of people from around the world representing hundreds of different religions. In this five-day conference, representatives of all of the world's religions gather in one place uniting in service to the same God in their various ways. Talk about a kaleidoscope! Whether addressing human trafficking, climate change, war/violence and hate, income inequality, or challenges of indigenous communities, people gathered without any labels other than a common interest in making the world a better place.

This is true with another group I have been introduced to, Idealists of the World. This is a global social media group made up of over 40,000 people from around the world. We unite online to support one another as we strive to improve our communities and look for connections for how to implement improvements. Idealists' motto is "Bridging the gap between intention and action."

One fall morning, prior to attending the 2018 Parliament, I kept hearing the words, "Let there be peace on earth. Let it begin with me" in my mind. I'm fairly certain it was a song I heard as there was a melody playing as well. I was pondering the necessity of labels. Should I be identifying with one group or another? If asked, what label would I give myself? While preparing to meditate, the essence Niaouli begged to be present. I asked Niaouli, "What do you have to share with me about this idea of labels?" The following is the message I received:

My gentle Earth-loving child, there is no need to identify yourself with any one particular sect or religion. You are a child of God, a child of the Creator of all things. Each time you assist a worm or teach others to love their "Wormy," you are expressing who you are. With each innocent creature you admire or help (like the goldfinch and butterfly) you are expressing who you are. Each time you offer to share what you've learned with those around you, you are expressing who you are. Love life and live your life to the fullest, and you are expressing who you are. Bless you, Earth Being!

I never thought about my common, everyday activities defining who I am. My grandchildren and I love playing in the dirt and finding worms. In her cute two-year-old voice, Ellie named her worm "Woomy". It came naturally for me to gently move the distraught goldfinch who had encountered a glass door and to send healing energy to a butterfly who seemed out of sorts. This beautiful message from nature was a wonderful reminder to simply love life to the fullest. No labels necessary.

Perhaps there are labels in your life that no longer serve a purpose. Are you ready to release them? Are you willing to release them?

If you were going to authentically identify yourself, what words would you choose?

Loving Kindness Goes a Long Way

"In every walk with nature one receives far more than he seeks."
John Muir (Muir, 2020)

Have you ever hurt someone unintentionally? I did. And it did not feel good at all. Thankfully, this was someone who felt comfortable enough to let me know. I had been teaching an aromatherapy class and had light-heartedly brought out this person's issues with controlling situations. Well, I thought it was light-hearted. She did not. And it hurt her. She made other accusations about things I had said in previous encounters, and I felt bad that I had been so insensitive toward her. I pondered this as I walked in nature and I was graced with a gift of a hawk feather. I believe Archangel Michael, who helps clear negativity and releases us from fear and doubt, was present and guided me to a loving response to this situation. I instantly began sending her loving kindness: May you be well. May you be happy. May you be at peace. May you be forgiving. May you feel my love.

Later, as I meditated with the ancient essence of Spikenard, this message came through:

This work isn't easy and it is not for the faint hearted. You are
strong and are called to do the difficult task of bringing oth-
ers to the place of their own sovereignty. Some are ready and
some will resist. Some who desire to be well aren't willing to
do the work to get there yet. These opportunities are making

you stronger. Do not doubt your mission. You are called to do this. Keep trusting as we are guiding you. Stand in your Truth and don't waiver. You cannot control others so trust that their journey is THEIR journey. Love them with all of your heart. Then there will be no room for doubts! You are not a failure and you did not succeed. It just is as it is. Love above all else.

Healing on all levels--physically, emotionally and spiritually--is a process. I cannot make anyone forgive me. I can only humble myself, admit my wrongdoings, and trust there is a lesson in each situation for all who are involved. Take a moment to reflect on a person or situation where you unintentionally hurt someone. It is never too late to come to a place of humility. Know you will become a stronger person, a person of integrity, if you can send that person unconditional loving kindness in whatever way is comfortable for you. This is how you become your authentic, sovereign self. This is who we are all meant to be.

Loving Kindness (Metta) is a Buddhist practice to develop impartial and unconditional love. Initially taught by the Buddha, it exists in most ancient spiritual disciplines: The following is a simplified version:

We begin by sending loving kindness to ourselves first:

May I be well. May I be happy. May I be peaceful. May I be forgiven for any wrongdoings I have done to myself or others. May I be free from suffering. (Repeat until you feel it.)

Once we feel love for ourselves, then we can send it out to others:

May you be well. May you be happy. May you be peace-ful. May you be forgiven for any wrongdoings you have done to yourself or others. May you be free from suffering.

You can do this for each person who comes to mind. Customize it to fit the loving kindness you wish to send out. You can take it one step further and offer it to people you don't know. And ultimately, to all the world. This practice is reported to reduce irritation, anger, and hatred, while improving patience and the ability to forgive. Think about what a wonderful world this would be if we all practiced loving kindness each day of our lives!

Slowing Down

"Adopt the pace of nature: her secret is patience."
Ralph Waldo Emerson (Emerson, 2020)

In the fast-paced society we live in, it is easy to get caught up in the day-to-day grind. If you have children, the activity list seems to be endless. If you have a career outside of the home, long hours can consume a good portion of your day. If you commute, there is another large chunk of time taken up. Not to mention the domestic obligations like cooking, cleaning, and laundry. Everything we engage in keeps time ticking away. By the end of the day, we collapse, exhausted from not having had time to replenish.

In 2019, I decided to move my massage practice and yoga class home. I converted a small office conveniently located near the entrance, and I created a beautiful yoga studio in my lower level. It felt like a dream come true. By no longer commuting, I added six to seven hours to my week plus another one to two hours per day in saved preparation/clean up time. It was a wonderful gift! Somehow, though, I still felt as though I always had to be working, doing something that had to be added to my calendar. Until these past months. Everything changed.

Due to the global pandemic we are experiencing, everything has come to a screeching halt. I removed everything from my calendar for the past few months, and it looks as though my calendar will remain empty for the next several months. Talk about being forced to slow down! In my journal, I came across the following message (written in 2018), I chuckled at how the Universe has stepped in to slow us all down. Here is the message the ancient essence Himalayan Soti opened me up to receive:

You are very good at listening to the messages we bring you. We want you to feel and live those messages deeply. Slow down. Spend time taking it all in. All experiences come forth to remind you to stand in your authenticity. Stand in what you believe to be true. Do not waiver or allow the lower energies of doubt or judgment to overtake you. You must come from a place of unconditional love and compassion with the understanding that everyone is on their own journey. You are a messenger but not responsible for others' choices to listen or not. Hear the messages, stand in your belief and authentic place, do not waiver. Believe what you are guided to say and do comes from a higher realm. We are a team and all receive eternal guidance from Source. You must believe and own this. No harm will come to you or those you serve as we come from a place of Divine Love. You have our blessing with you always. Release judgment, embrace who you are, and walk this journey with joy and gratitude in your heart.

This stay-at-home order isn't exactly how we would all like life to be, but it is noteworthy. My prayer now is for the majority of people to see this as a wake-up call and use this opportunity to re-evaluate their lives. My husband and I have seen more children playing outside in our neighborhood in this past month than we've seen in the fourteen years we've lived here. We see more couples and families walking or bicycling together on the trails, keeping their safe distance, of course.

As I ponder the above message, I, too, am reminded of the importance of slowing down. It's okay to have an empty calendar. It's okay to just sit and contemplate. It's okay to be an observer of nature and the beings occupying this beautiful planet. By slowing down, I feel more grounded and present than I have ever felt. I am reminded of a passage I learned in a Bible study group: *"No testing has overtaken you that is not common to everyone. God is faithful, and he will not let you be tested beyond your strength, but with the testing he will also provide the way out so that you may be able to endure it." 1 Corinthians 10:13 (NRSV)*

By slowing down, I have been able to endure the ominous pandemic consuming the attention of the entire world. I am able to find gratitude for the simple task of being able to take a breath. I am able to reach out with love and compassion to those who come to mind during my contemplative moments.

Have you been able to take the time to slow down?

If not, is there something on your calendar that really doesn't NEED to be there?

What new insights have come your way when you have slowed down?

What messages of authenticity have you been ignoring?

Meditation

Becoming Your Authentic Self

The intention for this meditation is to heal, restore, and align our solar plexus chakra. Draw your attention to the solar plexus, the space a little above the navel and slightly below the sternum: the place where empowerment, personal power, confidence, and knowing your authentic place in the world all reside. The element associated with this chakra is fire, the type of fire that ignites who you are meant to be.

If this chakra is blocked, digestive issues or feelings of low self-worth may be present. Shame is generally responsible for the imbalance. Too much of our power is given away to others, or to situations in the workplace or at home. We lack self-confidence. We question and doubt ourselves. We never feel we are good enough. Decisions are difficult for us to make. In order for our energy centers to flow freely, it is imperative that we reclaim who we truly are and who we are meant to be.

Let's begin, taking in some slow, deep, cleansing breaths. Draw your attention inward and release all thoughts and concerns that may be lingering in your mind. For this practice, focus on the area slightly above your navel as your diaphragm expands with the in-breath and contracts with the out-breath, feeling a gentle rise and fall as you follow each breath. Use the out-breath to release all that doesn't serve you in this moment.

Focusing on your solar plexus imagine a beautiful, vibrant, glowing yellow flame in the very center. First, use this beautiful flame to burn away all of the ways you have given away your personal power. One by one ceremoniously place them in the fire thanking them for the purpose they served, letting them know they are no longer needed, observing how the flame grows bigger and brighter each time something is released and burned away.

Now this bright, beautiful flame ignites and releases a power within you that has always been there. Take time to welcome this powerful energy. Embrace it! Enjoy your reconnection to your true nature, your authenticity. Feel this gentle but bold energy filling you with excitement and anticipation for what is to come next for you.

Slowly bring your awareness back to your space, feeling the confidence and courage this experience has brought you … be aware that this beautiful yellow energy is surrounding you and expanding out in all directions, bask in the joy and freedom this brings. Know you are empowered to do anything your heart is calling you to do.

When you are ready, slowly open your eyes. See life from this empowered place of authenticity.

Essential Oil Message
Review from Chapter 3

Authenticity

Rosemary, Verbenone

You are as unique and beautiful as the vibrant patterns in a kaleidoscope. As you breathe in, each of your cells shifts and changes, and as you exhale, they change again. Through the eyes of nature, all of creation is seen in this beautiful way. As with a kaleidoscope, when the light is obstructed or fades, the vibrancy dims. The colors and shapes are still there but are not as prevalent. This is true with humans as well. Sometimes you encounter circumstances that may dim or shadow your vibrancy. It is still there. It just needs a little light to shine through and bring it back to its full glory. Remember this when you encounter people who are struggling. Shine some light on their kaleidoscopes so they can see their vibrancy once again. Using Rosemary helps you remember the Divine, beautiful, colorful kaleidoscope you are! Peace be with you!

Sage True

I am here to support you and to take you deeper into your understanding. Stay focused on sharing your Truth. You have been, are, and will be touching many lives. Everyone who hears you is taking in the seeds you are planting. Some will grow slower than others. Keep planting! You have been plucking out the weeds that were stunting your growth. Do not ruminate over them. Let them go. Thank them for the part they played in your life and then release them.

Niaouli

My gentle Earth-loving child, there is no need to identify your-self with any one particular sect or religion. You are a child of God, a child of the Creator of all things. Each time you assist a worm or teach others to love their "Wormy," you are expressing who you are. Through each innocent creature you admire or help (like the goldfinch and butterfly), you are expressing who you are. Each time you offer to share what you've learned with those around you, you are expressing who you are. Love life and live your life to the fullest. You are expressing who you are. Bless you, Earth Being!

Spikenard

This work isn't easy and it is not for the faint hearted. You are strong and are called to do the difficult task of bringing others to the place of their own sovereignty. Some are ready and some will resist. Some who desire to be well aren't willing to do the work to get there yet. These opportunities are making you stronger. Do not doubt your mission. You are called to do this. Keep trusting as we are guiding you. Stand in your Truth and don't waiver. You cannot control others, so trust that their journey is THEIR journey. Love them with all of your heart. Then there will be no room for doubts! You are not a failure and you did not succeed. It just is as it is. Love above all else.

Himalayan Soti

You are very good at listening to the messages we bring you. We want you to feel and live those messages deeply. Slow down. Spend time taking it all in. All experiences come forth to remind you to stand in your authenticity. Stand in what you believe to be true. Do not waiver or allow the lower energies of doubt or judgment to overtake you. You must come from a place of unconditional love and compassion with the understanding that everyone is on their own journey.

You are a messenger but not responsible for others' choices to listen or not. Hear the messages, stand in your belief and authentic place, do not waiver. Believe that what you are guided to say and do comes from a higher realm. We are a team and all receive eternal guidance from Source. You must believe and own this. No harm will come to you or those you serve as we come from a place of Divine Love. You have our blessing with you always. Release judgment, embrace who you are, and walk this journey with joy and gratitude in your heart.

Nature's Choir

Listen … can you hear the singing?

The crickets with their steady rhythm keeping the choir together

The birds chirping in their melodious tones

The wind whistling through the leaves

The waves clapping at nature's perfect song

Harmonizing with the sounds of nature.

-2012

Chapter 4

Mindfulness

*"Those who find beauty in all of nature
will find themselves at one with the secrets of life itself."*
L. Wolfe Gilbert (Gilbert, 2020)

Enjoy Life in This Moment

Mindfulness is the practice of paying attention in the present moment, and doing it intentionally with non-judgment. Mindfulness meditation practices refer to the deliberate acts of regulating attention through the observation of thoughts, emotions, and body states.

The concept of mindfulness was foreign to me prior to beginning my healing work. I had a habit of multitasking, my mind going in many different directions at once. It is no wonder much of my life flew by in a blur. I'm really not sure why I went from being such a contemplative child to a crazed adult, but I'm guessing I needed to be on that path in order to bring me to where I am now in life, which is one of slow-paced mindfulness.

Once I started to meditate and practice mindfulness, I began to see and hear things I had not noticed in the past. If I heard an unfamiliar bird's song, I'd be drawn to finding that unique creature. I began looking at the land around me and noticing the diversity of colors and the contrast of the various landforms surrounding me. I began to be more aware of the ebb and flow of life and how it correlated to nature. I began to listen to the still small voice within.

I also started noticing people and how they moved and navigated through life. Several summers ago, while visiting my son in Connecticut, I spent five days of blissful mindfulness. I wrote, I painted, I contemplated life. My son was quite concerned. He encouraged me to explore New York City while he was at work. He suggested I spend the day visiting museums. To him, it appeared I was bored when actually I was more content than I had ever been. Practicing mindfulness in *being* rather than *doing* was not something he understood at that time.

In our fast-paced, multifunctioning world, it is a foreign concept to be mindful. We are such a production-driven society--always doing and rarely being--that being contemplative seems to be a waste of time. I've even witnessed trainers of the program, "Mindfulness Based Stress Reduction" living a life of constant doing, always on the move. Until now.

COVID-19, has brought the entire world to a halt. Wait, is it possible? Indeed, it is. Throughout this pandemic, people from all over the world are experiencing what it is like to be still as many have been confined to their homes for several months. It is an uncomfortable, unfamiliar feeling to be present with only yourself and perhaps your loved ones. People are getting edgy and bored, anxious for things to get back to "normal" (living in the past). The media wants to keep us updated on current conditions, which can easily lead us into the "what-if's" and making all kinds of assumptions (living in the future). We are all being called to be mindful and present with each choice and decision we make in this moment. We are called to live and enjoy this present moment. I turned to a message that came through when I was using my Lemon essential oil:

Enjoy life and all it brings to you! The pulsing vibrations you are experiencing come from lemon's stimulating power. Remember to be present and alive in every moment. Too often humans walk through life unaware. Many are waking up, but not fully. The habit or pattern of doing things in a daze has become very strong. Even those who are "awake" slip into patterns of complacency. Be mindful of this! Bring my essence out periodically to help you remember to stay fresh and alive in every moment. Enjoy ALL of your experiences. Change your routine. Step out in nature when you wake up and before ending your day.

My family has a new routine in pandemic times. My son talks to me frequently these days. He shared with me his experience of gazing out the window while working from home. He noticed the variety of birds each day changed. He watched their mating routines and was fascinated by the rituals they go through. I have been able to manifest what I would consider my perfect day by starting my day in contemplation, tending to my gardens, observing the changes in nature as I have found more time to cycle and hike, and nourishing my body with a plant-based diet. When I get pulled into the frenzy of the happenings in the world, I turn to a simple mindfulness practice Thich Nhat Hanh shares in his book, Be Free Where You Are (Hanh, 2002). Thay, as his followers affectionately call him, is a Buddhist monk who has written many inspirational books. Here is an excerpt:

> Breathing in, I know I am breathing in.
>
> Breathing out, I know I am breathing out.
>
> Breathing in, I notice that my in-breath has become deeper.
>
> Breathing out, I notice that my outbreath has become slower.
>
> Breathing in, I calm myself.
>
> Breathing out, I feel at ease.
>
> Breathing in, I smile.
>
> Breathing out, I release.
>
> Breathing in, I dwell in the present moment.
>
> Breathing out, I feel it is a wonderful moment.
>
> In, Out; Deep, Slow;
>
> Calm, Ease; Smile, Release;
>
> Present Moment, Wonderful Moment.

Now is the time to start fresh and to live from a place of mindfulness in every moment, enjoying every experience no matter how difficult or challenging it may seem. None of us can predict the future and we have never known how long we will be occupying this planet, so why not enjoy each moment we have been given?

When your day-to-day routine changes unexpectedly, are you able to relax into the flow?

Do you find yourself grasping onto memories from the past or feeling apprehensive about the uncertain future?

What shifts can you make to bring you back to your center?

Dreams Awaken Our Senses

I tend to have vivid dreams. I dream in color, and I remember many details once awake. Occasionally, when a dream feels profound, I write it down in my dream journal. There is one recurring element that weaves through many of my dreams. Invariably, I am going somewhere, either walking or driving, and I have the sensation that I cannot open my eyes. It is as if my eyes are so heavy and tired, I can't even hold them open with my fingers. In these dreams, I'm focused on this handicap of not being able to open my eyes. I'm not overly frightened, just frustrated. Somehow, I know what is around me but I am aware I cannot use my eyes to see. The result is that I usually wake myself up. This particular repetitive dream has me stumped. I have not consulted a dream expert, but my hunch is it has something to do with relying too much on my physical vision rather than my intuitive vision. Spikenard, the ancient sacred anointing essence, shed some light on this subject:

> *You rely very much on your senses as you know them. You are encouraged to see with your ears, hear with your eyes, feel with your ears and eyes, see with your heart, and so on. And you are ready to go deeper with this. The world's sacred texts encourage releasing any attachment to your senses and that is what prefaces becoming more intuitive and less reliant on your senses. Re-read this daily as your reminder. From this place of non-attachment, you will find you judge less and you become more compassionate.*

Our senses are part of our human experience. On one hand, they are very useful when we are taking in our surrounding environment. On the other hand, we may become overly reliant on our senses. I had a student in my preschool classroom who was visually impaired. She was considered legally blind as she had no vision in front of her and she had very little peripheral vision. At the request of her mom, I welcomed her into our classroom even though I wasn't a certified Special Ed teacher. This experience taught me a lot about how we can become dependent on one particular sense, in this case, vision. As her teacher, I had to make sure I always kept the classroom safe. This meant I could no longer rearrange the furniture or bring something new into the classroom without first taking Meghan by the hand and showing her the new item by having her touch and feel it slowly, imprinting it in her memory. She also taught me to be more in tune to my other senses, especially hearing and touch. After playing in the tactile area, where I had put out salt in a shallow box for the children to practice writing their name, Meghan came up to me and insisted I touch her hands. She was delighted at how soft they were after playing in the salt.

Our senses serve to guide us when we're making decisions. What would happen if we intentionally chose not to use them? In some of the Eastern traditions, we are taught to let go of attachment to our senses (for instance, sounds outside of our space that may distract us from our meditation or seeing food on commercials and thinking we need to eat). The practice is to notice them but not allow our thoughts to attach to them.

One beneficial practice is to use one of your senses that doesn't automatically engage in a situation. Close your eyes and use your sense of sound to "see" your surroundings. What comes to your awareness first? Put your earbuds in and watch others around you. Can you sense what they might be saying or feeling without hearing their tone?

These practices can help you to open up the pathway to your own intuition. Our intuition is always there. We simply need to tune into it. By the way, have you ever tried playing in salt with your hands? Try it!

Integrating Mindfulness

I have been blessed with many wonderful experiences and learning opportunities throughout my life. During the years I was a preschool director, the staff and I received a grant designated for continuing education. All of us felt a calling to deepen the spiritual teachings we offered the children, and we were serendipitously led to a training in a program entitled "Young Children and Worship". This took place in Holland, Michigan, and it was led by the author of the book of the same title, Sonja Stewart. The program blended the philosophies of Maria Montessori and Sophia Cavaletti and engaged the children as they heard the Bible stories. We implemented the program the following school year, and it became a regular part of our spiritual development curriculum for our students.

At the same time, I implemented the program, known as "Worship Center," on Sunday mornings for the children of our congregation. The beauty of the program was how it integrated mindfulness into the style of teaching. Instead of feeding the children information and expecting them to retain it, it engaged them in responding to the stories through deep wondering, action, and awareness of what was going on in their world at the time. For example, in one story Jesus says, "Come. Follow me. I will show you the way of the kingdom of God. Heal the sick. Care for the poor. Embrace the widows. And enjoy the children." In response to this story, the children made healing prayer crosses and they gave them to people in our community who were in need of healing. Each week we remembered to include those individuals in our prayers, and often the children told me they were praying for them at home too. The children also sent cards and letters to a child in Haiti whom we adopted through Compassion International and to some of our members who were imprisoned. It was a beautiful way of being mindful of the world. I loved being a part of that program. The beauty of the children's pure and natural spirituality touched my heart deeply.

I thought our children's Worship Center would go on forever, but it didn't. The world around us was beginning to change, and one by one the families moved on to discover their own faith path. We held on until there was only one family left. Then the program dissolved, leaving the church with no program for children.

Often, as I sit and meditate, the stories I told the children will come to mind. There were so many layers to the teachings of Jesus it isn't surprising when they surface to bring an awareness or lesson to me. I wonder if I'll ever have the opportunity to share these stories again. I wonder if there is a new venue in which to tell them. One morning, Rosemary carried forward a message:

Remember all of God's creation is with you at all times and through all situations. Keep that in the forefront of your mind. Listen to others and you will be guided IF something needs to be spoken. Always ask for guidance first. Open your heart like Jesus did. Keep his teachings close to your heart and live them! We love you and are excited to be on this journey with you! Blessings abound indeed.

As I pondered this message, I remembered how connected I felt to my path and how much joy and gratitude filled my heart. As you reflect on your life, in what ways can you see that mindfulness was present, even if you weren't aware at the time?

What emotions does your memory recall?

How can we use these recollections as fuel to feed us on our current path?

Stand Solid Where You Are

"If we surrendered to earth's intelligence, we could rise up rooted like trees." Rainer Maria Rilke (Macy, 2005)

Oftentimes, when I am going through a transition period in my life, I want to flee, to run away to some place unknown and start fresh, leaving behind all that has troubled me. I'm not 100 per cent sure, but I would venture to guess this happens to many people. Sometimes, it feels as though it would be easier to start over than to muddle my way through the void. Of course, this doesn't actually happen. I have too many reasons to stay where I am, namely my two beautiful grandchildren whom I love and adore, my clients, and my extended family. I have found this momentary desire to flee occurs when I've neglected to stay mindful and have allowed my mind to wander into the land of "what-if's" and "if-only's." Guaiacwood, a salve-like essence from Paraguay, was one I chose on a day I was experiencing this type of funk. She fulfilled her role and took me deep into my meditation:

Stand solid where you are, Beloved. You must release your constant thoughts about moving away from where you live. Be present and find joy where you are as this is exactly where you need to be in this moment. The tree world doesn't experience such desires. We are happy to be wherever we are and enjoy life as it is. You stand in judgment of those who you don't think are awake in life. That is why you are called to be there! Be the Light that awakens them. Live from your place of authenticity and don't worry about how others perceive you. The universe knows where you need to be and before another opportunity opens, you must embrace the lessons now! Release all judgments!

I'll admit it, sometimes I argue with God: *"But I want to be around open-minded people. I'm too angry to shine my Light. Why did you plop me in the middle of a corn field? I've tried to show the way, only to be rejected and mocked."* And then something shifts and mindfulness brings me back to the present moment where I can stand solid in who I am with the understanding that I have the choice to be where I want to be. I am grateful for the essences and the reminders they bring. I am grateful that I am surrounded by nature and can breathe fresh air (except for the times the farmer spreads his manure). I am grateful for the opportunities to connect with like-minded people in other ways. I am grateful for the lives I have been able to touch. I love who I am and what I believe to be true. And what is most certainly true is that I know there *is* unconditional love holding and guiding me through all of life's challenges and lessons.

Have you ever had the feeling of wanting to run and start over?

What has carried you through those troubling times?

Next time it strikes, can you imagine yourself like a tree, standing solid in who you are and what you believe to be true?

Can you find joy in shining your Light where you currently are?

Meditation

Becoming Mindful

The intention for this meditation is to heal, restore, and align our Third Eye Chakra, also known as the Brow Chakra. This chakra brings us peace of mind and inner guidance. When we learn to access our insight and intuition, we have clearer thoughts and are able to direct our focus on our next actions.

When this chakra is blocked, you may experience pain through headaches, or pressure in the sinuses; you may simply feel foggy or blocked; you may experience confusion, scattered thoughts, doubts or frustration or you may have a difficult time concentrating.

Trust and surrender are accessed through this chakra. Clearing your brow chakra, you gain better concentration and hear the subtle messages from your higher self. When your mind calms, you find inspiration for the next step toward your dreams, accessing wisdom and guidance.

Begin centering yourself by bringing your focus to your breath … your life-giving breath. As you feel the rise and fall with each breath, allow your thoughts to drift through … and notice how your body begins to relax and let go. Be aware of any areas that might be holding on to tension … breathe deeply and gently … feeling a sense of release with each breath cycle.

Bring your awareness to the space between your brows … envision a deep violet or indigo light evolving and pulsing … it may even resemble the image of an eye. As this pulsing light grows … notice a beam reaching out into the darkness of space. With each pulse, sense you are being fully and completely connected to your source of life …

an inner knowing that all is well emerges … you experience complete trust and you surrender to this peaceful, connected feeling.

Basking in this brilliant, pulsing energy … you realize messages are coming to you … images … words … a knowingness stronger and bolder than you've ever experienced. Allow these messages to flow through to you without attaching to any of them … you see this beautiful, effortless guidance coming through … you feel inspired and connected to a Divine plan. This beautiful energy is surrounding you with the brilliant violet/indigo light.

Mindfully bring your awareness back to your breath. Settle into your body and experience a deeper sense of your own highest guidance. You clearly see your next actions.

Slowly open your eyes and embrace the vision of this mindfulness moment.

Essential Oil Message
Review from Chapter 4

Mindfulness

Lemon

Enjoy life and all it brings to you! The pulsing vibrations you are experiencing come from lemon's stimulating power. Remember to be present and alive in every moment. Too often humans walk through life unaware. Many are partly waking up, but not fully. The habit or pattern of doing things in a daze has become very strong. Even those who are "awake" slip into patterns of complacency. Be mindful of this! Bring my essence out periodically to help you remember to stay fresh and alive in every moment. Enjoy ALL of your experiences. Change your routine. Step out in nature at the beginning and the ending of each day.

Spikenard

You rely very much on your senses as you know them. You are encouraged to broaden your use of those senses--see with your ears, hear with your eyes, feel with your ears and eyes, see with your heart, and so on. And you are ready to go deeper with this. The world's sacred texts encourage releasing any attachment to your senses and that is what prefaces becoming more intuitive and less reliant on your senses. Re-read this daily as your reminder. From this place of non-attachment, you will find you judge less and you become more compassionate.

Rosemary Verbenone

Remember all of God's creation is with you at all times and through all situations. Keep that in the forefront of your mind. Listen to others and you will be guided IF something needs to be spoken. Always ask for guidance first. Open your heart like Jesus did. Keep his teachings close to your heart and live them! We love you and are excited to be on this journey with you! Blessings abound indeed.

Guaiacwood

Stand solid where you are, Beloved. You must release your constant thoughts about moving away from where you live. Be present and find joy where you are as this is exactly where you need to be in this moment. The tree world doesn't experience such desires. We are happy to be wherever we are and enjoy life as it is. You stand in judgment of those who you don't think are awake in life. That is why you are called to be there! Be the Light that awakens them. Live from your place of authenticity and don't worry about how others perceive you. The universe knows where you need to be, and before another opportunity opens, you must embrace the lessons now! Release all judgments!

Drought 2012

Thirsty land, parched and dry

Drinking up whatever rain it can

Fields of cornstalks, stunted and dry

Food for many living beings not being produced by Mother Nature

Have we caused this phenomenon?

Greedily using Her resources

Forgetting our gratitude

Forgetting to give back to our precious, sacred Earth

So many people facing personal droughts

Labor cut-backs, lower income

Many losing their life-work passion

Wandering, floundering

Searching for direction

Lacking motivation to move forward

Ever so slowly

Adjusting to a new way of being

Let go of what was

Embrace the present

Our Creator will never abandon us.

-2012

Chapter 5

Acceptance

*"In nature, nothing is perfect and everything is perfect.
Trees can be contorted, bent in weird ways,
and they're still beautiful." Alice Walker* (Walker, 2020)

Judgment: The Opposite of Acceptance

I understand that judgment is human nature. It has always been one of those things I cringe at in others. I'm not talking about using good judgment here. I'm referring to the many layers of how judgment is used to measure someone or something. It is an automatic response that promotes comparison and superiority. We must become mindful of its presence in order to move in the opposite direction towards acceptance, compassion, and understanding. What I have learned throughout my healing years is that recognizing it in others is only the first step. Yikes! I began seeing all of the ways I, too, stood in judgment…like judging those who were judging others. What a vicious circle that is! As I began to reflect and heal the layers of judgment I had, I turned to Artemisia Titepati, a beautiful, pungent essence, to assist me:

Surrender to the unconditional love of the Universe. People have many threads of judgment holding them back from experiencing this love completely. Each time you become aware of judging, name it and recognize it as it is no longer serving your higher purpose. Cut that cord. Remember each person is on their own journey and it doesn't mean they are worse than you or behind in their evolvement. It just is what it is. Send them loving thoughts. This is how you will begin to experience the unconditional love of the Universe.

I realized I had been judging a dear friend of mine. She was someone I admired and had been a beautiful teacher in my life. This time she was bringing me a different kind of lesson, unbeknown to her. She, too, is on a healing path and isn't perfect. I was reminded of how much I allowed her comments and feelings to disturb my peace. This led to an internal judgment battle. I learned through this experience that instead of me standing in judgment of her journey, I could bless her and send her love for showing me how we approach our businesses differently. No judgment. Just recognition. I also learned a healthier way to deflect those situations is to protect myself by placing a shield of Divine love around me. When I feel loved and confident, others' remarks won't have the opportunity to take hold.

When I began my healing journey, I learned the Serenity Prayer … "God, grant me the serenity to accept the things I cannot change, courage to change the things I can, and wisdom to know the difference." This beautiful gift the universe taught me is that in true acceptance of the things I cannot change (others), I am free from the lure of judgment. Of course, I've had multiple opportunities to practice this lesson and continue to return to it as needed.

I encourage you to take time to notice when you are caught in the trap of judging others. This may take practice. Be open to humbly examining your thoughts and messages. Reflect on the following questions:

Just because this is true for me, does it mean it must be true for others?

How can I see _____ through the eyes of love and compassion?

Does my way of perceiving this have to be the right way? Why?

Acceptance Moves Us from Exhaustion to Exhilaration

Throughout learning the lessons of acceptance and releasing judgment, which I now realize is a life-long process, I found myself working through some unhealthy attachments to judgment in my sleep. I dreamed about people and places and their particular situations. This brought restless sleep and I woke not feeling refreshed at all. Davana brought me clarity with these challenges:

When you are feeling responsible for others' situations and a bit guilty, remember these are lower vibrations lingering. Release each person and each situation by sending them love and Divine Light, and know their journey is exactly that ...THEIR journey. Release without judgment. Acceptance of another's path involves truly loving them where they are. Yes, this applies to ALL. You are crossing the bridge to another way of existence; however, you are stuck on the bridge waiting for others to cross with you. What are you afraid of? Loneliness? Remember, your Creator exists within you. Isolation? You are

71

ceaselessly surrounded by Divine Holy Love. Doubt? Trust and believe. Allow yourself to move forward and have faith that every experience is there for a purpose. Relax into total acceptance. Your inner guidance is present to help you move from exhaustion to exhilaration!

Exhilaration sounds good to me. How about you? As you are working through your layers toward acceptance, take a moment to reflect:

Imagine you are on a bridge crossing to another way of existence. On one side of the bridge is life as you've known it, full of judging others and populated by everyone who has participated in judging one way or another. On the other side, life is free from judgment and full of joy and abundant, unconditional love. Everyone here accepts one another exactly as they are.

Do you feel stuck on the bridge? If so, what is preventing you from taking the next step forward in your life?

What are you afraid of? Could it be loneliness, isolation, or judgment?

Do you have doubts? Reread the message from Davana and take her message into your heart.

Breaking Old Patterns Through Healing the Chakras

If you are new to the Chakras, there are many wonderful sources of information that can introduce you to these energy centers that give us windows into our personal healing. I often will be drawn to begin my meditation time with the practice of balancing each of the chakras, especially if I'm feeling a bit off center.

On one particular morning, I was drawn to bring my fingertips on both hands together to allow the flow of energy to have a continuous current. I started with the Root Chakra, earth element and belonging. I felt assured that I belong where I am. Next, I went to the Sacral Chakra, water element and pro-creation of life and work. I felt residual guilt present relating to money and I cleared that away. Upon arriving at the Solar Plexus Chakra, fire element, there was a presence of anger and shame, especially around judgment. These were here to remind me to continue to revisit this area and go inward to release areas of judgment that have crept in. At the Heart Chakra, air element, I felt a block to deep love and acceptance of all, especially with my husband. Wild Tansy was the essence I chose to assist me. Her message was direct and firm:

My desire is to assist you in feeling a sense of belonging in this life. Release any attachments to guilt, anger, and shame; especially with judgment. These are present to help you go inward and release. Deep love and acceptance are available to all. Our desire is for this to be fully-present in each human being. Any of your resistance to others is what is blocking their desire to expand. Your agitation stirs up insecurities within those on the receiving end that they are not aware of. They will then respond in ways that are familiar to them: blaming, shaming, anger, etc. In those moments it is crucial that you fully embrace them with an open, loving heart. That is how others will begin to see. They first need to experience it, over and over again just like you did. Vulnerability is not an easy place for humans to exist. That is also your lesson. When you feel attacked, it is your indication you are holding onto an old pattern. Use this as an opportunity to send unconditional love. When others need constant reassurance of your love, this is a mirror for you to see that you are not fully expressing your love. Become totally aware of this process. Open your heart even more!

Wow! What an impactful message. I was prepared to do the work necessary to break the old patterns. Using the essences is a powerful way to bring forth emotions, situations, and people that we need to release and heal. Using the mirror to reflect back the emotions we are currently facing is another beneficial tool. Take a moment to ponder what your mirror is reflecting back to you. Use the following summary of the Chakras to help identify areas within your body where you might be storing old emotional patterns. Journal your responses and come back to them as often as needed until those old patterns dissolve. Remember, in order to truly replace an old pattern, we must confidently embrace a new pattern.

Chakra	Position	Central Issue	Adversary
Root	base of spine	Survival	Fear
Sacral	below navel	Sexuality, Emotions	Guilt
Solar Plexus	above navel	Power, Energy	Shame
Heart	center of chest	Love	Grief
Throat	hollow of throat	Communication	Lies
Third Eye	between the eyebrows	Intuition, Imagination	Illusion
Crown	top of head	Awareness	Attachment

Meditation

Radiating Love and Acceptance

Bring your focus to the Heart Chakra. This energy center governs the heart, lungs and circulatory system. It includes the shoulders, arms, and hands and is considered the gateway to the higher chakras. When this chakra is open, love flows through you easily and effortlessly ... giving and receiving love with ease. You are comfortable in all your relationships and you feel a heartfelt sense of gratitude for how wonderful your life is. You appreciate others and feel compassion for yourself and others without feeling sorry for anyone. You are one with life and accept all that is.

The central issue with the Heart Chakra is grief. If this chakra is imbalanced, you may feel as if you need to please others to be loved, you may have been hurt by others many times in relationships and now feel that you have to guard yourself from being hurt. You may feel afraid of commitment.

Let's begin by bringing your awareness to your breath as you settle in. Feel your chest expand as you take those slow deep breaths in, and as you exhale release all that isn't serving your highest good in this moment. Slowly count to 6 on the in-breath ... 1 ... 2 ... 3 ... 4 ... 5 ... 6 hold briefly before you allow the lungs to exhale even more slowly ...1 ... 2 ... 3 ... 4 ... 5 ... 6...7...8... pause before starting the process again. Be aware of the rise and fall of the chest.

Imagine you are standing in a radiant, lush green forest. Take in the beauty surrounding you: brilliant shades of green, wildflowers of vibrant varieties, birds and butterflies flitting about. Listen to the gentle sounds of nature: birds chirping, insects buzzing, leaves rustling

75

in the breeze, all invoking a sense of coming home. You look ahead and see a path beckoning you to follow it. As you saunter forward, you feel enveloped by the unconditional love of nature. Observing a soft, grassy clearing ahead, you find a comfortable place to rest. Surrounding you, this beautiful green energy pulses with love. Just as nature lives harmoniously with one another, you too, feel harmonious and full of love: for yourself, for the beauty surrounding you, for the amazing grace of being alive. Pausing, you take in this loving energy. You become aware of the sound of a stream nearby and you are drawn to it. As you stand at the water's edge, you see some leaves near your feet. Stooping, you pick one up, whisper a prayer, and release one of your blocks to fully loving yourself. You let go of the leaf and allow the wind to carry it to the stream. It gently moves out of your sight. Notice how you feel lighter, happier. And as other blocks to love come to mind, you continue to do this ceremony: whispering a prayer of release, letting the leaf gently flow out of your sight, until you feel so much lighter you could float away! You make your way back to the grassy clearing. You rest here, bathing in the unconditional love radiating from your heart … a beautiful, Divine green energy is surrounding you. You are full of peace.

Gently bring yourself back to our space. You know now that unconditional love, peace and acceptance are only a breath away! When you are ready, open your eyes.

Essential Oil Message
Review from Chapter 5

Acceptance

Artemisia, Titepati

Surrender to the unconditional love of the Universe. People have many threads of judgment holding them back from experiencing this love completely. Each time you become aware of judging, name it and recognize it as it is no longer serving your higher purpose. Cut that cord. Remember each person is on their own journey and it doesn't mean they are worse than you or behind in their evolvement. It just is what it is. Send them loving thoughts. This is how you will begin to experience the unconditional love of the Universe.

Davana

When you are feeling responsible for others' situations and a bit guilty, remember these are lower vibrations lingering. Release each person and each situation by sending them love and Divine Light, and know their journey is exactly that ...THEIR journey. Release without judgment. Acceptance of another's path involves truly loving them where they are. Yes, this applies to ALL. You are crossing the bridge to another way of existence; however, you are stuck on the bridge waiting for others to cross with you. What are you afraid of? Loneliness? Remember, your Creator exists within you. Isolation? You are ceaselessly surrounded by Divine Holy Love. Doubt? Trust and believe. Allow yourself to move forward and have faith that every experience is there for a purpose. Relax into total acceptance. Your inner guidance is present to help you move from exhaustion to exhilaration!

Tansy, Wild

My desire is to assist you in feeling a sense of belonging in this life. Release any attachments to guilt, anger, and shame; especially with judgment. These are present to help you go inward and release. Deep love and acceptance are available to all and desires to be fully-present in each human being. Any of your resistance to others is what is blocking their desire to expand. Your agitation stirs up insecurities within those on the receiving end that they are not aware of. They will then respond in ways that are familiar to them: blaming, shaming, anger, etc. In those moments it is crucial that you fully embrace them with an open, loving heart. That is how others will begin to see. They first need to experience acceptance, over and over again, just as you did. Vulnerability is not an easy place for humans to exist. That is also your lesson. When you feel attacked, it is your indication you are holding onto an old pattern. Use this as an opportunity to send unconditional love. When others need constant reassurance of your love, this is a mirror for you to see that you are not fully expressing your love. Become totally aware of this process. Open your heart even more!

Standing Rock Reservation

Rolling hills with buttes rising

Mile after secluded mile from civilization

Hot, dry, barren land

Small towns of hope

Holding the grief of many generations

Longing to be heard

Wanting to experience compassion from others

Hurting hearts, strong hearts

Seeking to follow their Creator's call

Rekindling connections to their heritage

Peacemakers striving to bring hope to their people

Touching lives that will never be the same.

-2012

Chapter 6

Surrender

"There is no will but God's. I seek his peace today."
A Course in Miracles *74.7:2-3* (Foundation for Inner Peace, 2007)

May My Will and Thy Will Be One

"Thy will be done, on Earth as it is in Heaven", was part of a prayer I recited more times than I can count. There are times when I wish I had studied the original languages of the Bible so I could understand the context in which this was written. I see Heaven differently than I did while being immersed in the teachings of my Missouri Synod Lutheran upbringing. I was raised to believe Heaven is where you go when you die, providing you are worthy. As I've said before, for many years I lived with the belief that I really had to earn my way, since I had made some not-so-good choices. But this idea of Heaven and Hell as two separate "places," one for the good and the other for the bad, doesn't serve me anymore.

In Buddhism, Nirvana would be the closest thing to Heaven, although Nirvana is a state of mind free from suffering, not a place. Don Miguel Ruiz, a descendent of the Toltec tradition from the ancient empire of Mexico, explains in his book The Four Agreements (Ruiz, 1997) heaven and hell are the conditions we create with our mind and if we learn to control the mind, similar to Buddhist teachings, we are living in Heaven. However, if we choose to latch on to the journeys the mind can take us on, the *mitote* as he calls it, we are choosing to live in Hell.

I don't know about you, but I certainly experience the place of Hell as Ruiz described. When this occurs, I realize I am more focused on *my* will rather than being in the flow of *Thy* will. Blue Yarrow brought a clear message forward:

> *Surrender into the flow of life. Surrender into nature. Surrender into your healing gifts. Surrender into the flow of writing. Just as nature surrenders to the seasons, so must you surrender to the process of unfolding. As solstices and equinoxes approach each year, reflect on the things you need to release and allow to die off. Just as nature releases the beauty she has held through the months of summer, she transitions with grace, dignity, and beauty. Know that you are supported. Trust and believe without a doubt.*

Take a few moments to reflect on any thoughts which perhaps are creating your personal *mitote*.

What do you need to release?

How can this transition be one of grace, dignity and beauty for you?

Now, reflect on the times when you have surrendered totally to the flow of life. How did that feel to you?

Were you surprised by the outcomes?

Once we surrender and are in the flow, the mind releases and becomes less disruptive, freeing us from our suffering.

Leading Without Imposing Your Will

From the Tao Te Ching #10:
"Can you love people and lead them without imposing your will?
... Giving birth and nourishing, having without possessing,
acting with no expectations, leading and not trying to control:
this is the supreme virtue." (Mitchell, 2013)

I have held several leadership roles throughout my adult life. In my early adult years, my self-esteem and self-confidence were non-existent, so I didn't really seek out being in charge. In most cases, I fell into the role or I was encouraged by others to take the lead. This often came with a price. I had clear visions for each task I took on, but lack of education and experience hindered me from leading fluently. I learned the hard knocks way. Humbly recognizing my shortcomings became my best friend, which was necessary for me, since I preferred things to unfold my way. The line from the Tao Te Ching above, *leading and not trying to control*, was foreign to me. My solar plexus chakra was totally out of balance, therefore I believed I needed to be in control in order to be an effective leader. I was wrong about that one! However, the more energetically balanced I became internally, the easier it was to release being in control. Instead, I led from a place of collaboration and cooperation, which helped me become a more effective organizer. The essence of Blue Spruce helped me to stand in my power and lead with grace and love. As I pondered the reading from the Tao, Blue Spruce brought forth this message:

Yes, Dear One, the wisdom of the sages rings true through-out all time. Lead by example. Keep this in the forefront of your mind. Those you lead may not show you that they are transforming, but you are significantly affecting them. Let go of attachment to outcomes.

The key for me to release my need to control all fell upon letting go of my perceived outcomes. I felt my leadership defined my self-worth, instead of trusting the input of others. Who's to say that my perceived outcome was the best? At times, we need to step back and surrender to the flow allowing situations to unfold organically. We have the opportunity to provide our loved ones, co-workers, friends, or students guidance but, at the same time, we should allow them to learn through trial and error. This process will open them to transform and blossom as they are ready.

Perhaps you are a leader. Are you able to lead without controlling? Have you examined your expectations? Are they realistic? Take time to carefully examine your motives and release any unhealthy attachments to outcomes. Or, perhaps you have encountered a leader who falls short of collaboration and cooperation. Rather than resisting their energy, it may be beneficial for you to lead by example in a quieter, but bolder way.

Seeing with Jesus' Eyes

One of the supervisory roles I've fulfilled several times is chaperoning mission trips for the youth of our church. My last youth trip, in 2012, was to McLaughlin, South Dakota, where we served the Lakota people on a Standing Rock reservation through a program called YouthWorks. We had two adults, myself and our Youth Director, Christine, and six teenagers. There were several other groups serving the same week we were there. Our day was broken into three segments with the morning and afternoon sessions immersed in service and the evening segment devoted to worship and team building. The YouthWorks team organized our five-day service opportunities, which included a variety of ways to support this reservation which was sorely in need of help in a multitude of ways. There was a day-camp offering activity to local children, there were dilapidated buildings in need of renovation, there was a ten-acre orchard in need of weeding and pruning, and there was a veteran's center where we engaged in activities with the resident veterans. The Bible passage theme for the week was Romans 12:1-12: *I appeal to you therefore, brothers and sisters, by the mercies of God, to present your bodies as a living sacrifice, holy and acceptable to God, which is your spiritual worship. Do not be conformed to this world, but be transformed by the renewing of your minds, so that you may discern what is the will of God—what is good and acceptable and perfect.... I say to everyone among you not to think of yourself more highly than you ought to think, but to think with sober judgment, each according to the measure of faith that God has assigned.... Let love be genuine; hate what is evil, hold fast to what is good; love one another with mutual affection; outdo one another in showing honor. Do not lag in zeal, be ardent in spirit, serve the Lord. Rejoice in hope, be patient in suffering, persevere in prayer.*

I include this here as it is pertinent to the experience that I am going to share with you. One of our first assignments was to write down on a bracelet one way we wanted to worship God through our actions in the upcoming week. We were asked to keep in mind that worship is about serving our purpose and to be mindful of our attitude behind what we were doing. I chose to write: *Open my heart to see with Jesus' eyes.* I had no idea what a powerful intention it would end up being.

This story is about Gerald. Gerald was one of the adult natives who battled substance abuse and was known for his hot temper and erratic behaviors. On our first day, my group was assigned to the Kids Club, which was held in the park across the street from our center. I loved working with children, so I was excited for this opportunity. However, given my organized, controlling self, I wasn't prepared for the unstructured nature of the day. First, we had 20 to 25 children who poured in from the surrounding area. Some of them came and went freely; many of them were victims of fetal alcohol syndrome and had very short attention spans; all of them craved attention. Our method for checking the kids in was to mark the back of their hands with numbers (indicating the city quadrant they lived in) and in colors that placed them in their age group. Many of the children eluded getting checked-in due to the imbalance of adult to child ratio. About midway through the afternoon, our YouthWorks counselor, Sam, approached me and cautioned me to keep my eye on a shirtless man (Gerald) who was slouched up against a tree about 50 yards away from my group. Fear began to creep in as the teacher in me tried desperately to keep things organized, all while I kept a watchful eye on our potential danger. Needless-to-say, I lost control when one child announced she needed to go potty. At the same time, many of the children needed assistance as they finished their project and one little girl said, "My brother and his friend just left." Yikes! As I sent one of our youth to alert the YouthWorks counselor to our situation, I noticed that Gerald was gone. Panic-stricken, I scanned the park and couldn't find him. I ended the day humbled and feeling as though I had failed in my leadership role.

Day two was better as only a handful of children came and the raucous boys didn't show up. There wasn't any sign of Gerald for most of the day, and the whole Kids Club flowed perfectly. About a half hour before the activity time ended, Sam engaged the children in a circle game. Twenty minutes into the game, Gerald plopped himself down just outside of the circle, a stone's-throw away from me. Barely able to get his words out, he looked at me and asked if he could take us to see Sitting Bull. Fortunately, Sam intervened and gracefully declined Gerald's offer. I was grateful for Sam's presence and ability to channel the situation.

Day three, my group was assigned to a worksite which needed a lot of prep work. Two hours into our day, we decided it would be best for me to take the youth back to our center for lunch, since the adults needed time to figure out a plan of action. As we sat enjoying our lunch under the cooling shade of a tree, Gerald once again plopped himself down, this time asking for a glass of water. One of the counselors obliged him and brought him a snack as well. Gerald's words were a little easier to comprehend, but his eyes were glassy and distant. He questioned me about a scripture that talked about Jesus speaking to the people who were supposed to be representing the church but were not welcoming others. At that moment, I looked down at the bracelet I had made on the first day and the words struck me, *"Open my heart to see with Jesus' eyes."* My heart was racing and fear tried to take hold, but I surrendered into the flow and responded to Gerald, "Ah, yes. The story about the hypocrites." Gerald nodded and began to share a part of his story; how the Christians were responsible for the death of his grandmother, how his people have suffered, how he wants to change things, how people don't understand. He told me he didn't want to harm anyone. I simply listened and nodded. It was all I could do; it was all God called me to do. My heart opened with compassion for this broken man as I surrendered to see with Jesus' eyes.

I had been caught up in fear and had neglected to pay attention to the scripture for the week from Romans 12:3: *For by the grace given to me I say to everyone among you not to think of yourself more highly than you ought to think, but to think with sober judgment.* It took a listening ear and an open heart for me to see Gerald as a fellow soul-journer on this path called life. Each opportunity we encounter brings us closer to *"what is the will of God—what is good and acceptable and perfect."* The beloved essence of Tamarack reminded me of this:

My dear child, you are living with one foot in each world, three-dimensional and beyond. Once you fully place both feet in the beyond, your internal struggle between the planes will be done. You are right. This all comes down to trust. Once you fully embrace that you are truly a magnificent being of Divine love, nothing anyone else says will matter because you will not have doubts anymore. Your self-confidence will be fully engaged and you will be able to stand in your power and allow others to stand in theirs. This is clearly a lesson for you to accept others where they are, without compromising where you are. Listen and learn from your seasoned teachers.

Surrendering to seeing Gerald through the eyes of compassion and understanding rather than fear and judgment was the key to unlock the higher vibrations of unconditional love and compassion. This heart-opening experience left a profound imprint on me. I believe this lesson was clearly brought forward at a time when I needed to surrender into a deeper level of trust. It is a good reminder for me to revisit this life-changing experience.

Are there moments in your life that have opened you to see through the lens of compassion and understanding?

What lower vibrations were preventing you from being in the flow of surrender?

How can the rhythms of life teach us to surrender?

Meditation

Surrendering Like a River

Find a comfortable position and begin focusing on your breath. Honor the time that you are giving yourself ... know you have all the time you need. Release any thoughts, worries or concerns that may be invading your mind.

Breathing in slowly, counting if it helps you to stay focused on the breath ... 1 – 2 – 3 – 4 ... Exhale slowly ... 1 – 2 – 3 – 4 ... Repeat this pattern until you feel totally present in this moment. Take time to honor and thank yourself for being right here, right now.

Sometimes, it may be difficult to release thoughts or concerns. If this is your challenge in this moment, honor and thank yourself for recognizing this. Find peace in the midst of wherever you are ... right here, right now.

Imagine you are floating gently down a river...allow yourself to let go and relax. Surrender as life's current carries you.

Hear the sweet songs of the birds, the quiet breeze rustling through the trees, the gentle lapping of the water as it brushes the shoreline.

Feel the warmth of the sun shining down ... smile and enjoy the peace of the moment.

Inhaling, you smell the fragrance of nature around you ... perhaps the smell of leaves ... or the fresh scent of pines ... or flowers ... or newly fallen rain ... whatever you are smelling brings you a feeling of belonging.

Look around you, what do you see? Who or what is there? Plants … or animals … or other beings? Gaze up and notice the white fluffy clouds floating by and the beautiful blue sky.

Gently place any distracting thoughts on a cloud and watch it drift by. Notice the gentle meandering of the river … and realize this is a reflection of your life … taking unexpected turns yet continuing to gently flow as long as you give in to the current and not resist. You are quiet … you are calm … you are gentle with yourself … you are peaceful.

This is the place where letting go can be found. This is the place of total surrender and acceptance. This is the place of restoring mind, body, and spirit. And all is good.

Gently bring your awareness back to the space you are in. Focus on your breath once again and begin to gently move your body. Feel the energy now coursing through every fiber of your body, filling you with balance. Find gratitude for the opportunity to let go and allow life to unfold exactly as it should. When you are ready, open your eyes.

Essential Oil Message Review from Chapter 6

Surrender

Blue Yarrow

Surrender into the flow of life. Surrender into nature. Surrender into your healing gifts. Surrender into the flow of writing. Just as nature surrenders to the seasons, so must you surrender to the process of unfolding. As solstices and equinoxes approach each year, reflect on the things you need to release and allow to die off. Just as nature releases the beauty she has held through the months of summer, she transitions with grace, dignity, and beauty. Know that you are supported. Trust and believe without a doubt.

Blue Spruce

Yes, Dear One, the wisdom of the sages rings true throughout all time. Lead by example. Keep this in the forefront of your mind. Those you lead may not show you that they are transforming, but you are significantly affecting them. Let go of attachment to outcomes.

Tamarack

My dear child, you are living with one foot in each world, three-dimensional and beyond. Once you fully place both feet in the beyond, your internal struggle between the planes will be done. You are right. This all comes down to trust. Once you fully embrace that you are truly a magnificent being of Divine love, nothing anyone else says will matter because you will not have doubts anymore. Your self-confidence will be fully engaged and you will be able to stand in your power and allow others to stand in theirs. This is clearly a lesson for you to accept others where they are, without compromising where you are. Listen and learn from your seasoned teachers.

Chapter 7

Divine Timing

*"My wish is to stay always like this,
living quietly in a corner of nature." Claude Monet* (Monet, 2020)

Manifestation of Visions

My first experience with bringing a vision I had into reality was over 30 years ago. My children were young. I was a stay-at-home mom and had been involved in a neighborhood Playgroup for both of my sons. Each mom took a turn being the host for three days in any given week. We gathered for three hours and balanced the time we had with the children between structured learning time, creative time, and free time. I enjoyed every aspect of implementing my week.

One year, my oldest didn't have anyone his age left in the group, so I decided to send him to a local preschool. This opportunity brought more inspiration to me. I used these inspirations with his younger brother and the group he was part of. I really missed being a Playgroup mom once my boys were school-age. When they were in school all day, our church added on a large multi-purpose room. Each of the committees were challenged to find ways the building could be used as outreach to the community during the week. I served on the Parish Education Committee, and I recommended we consider a half-day preschool program. Of course, I had no idea where to begin, but really felt like I was being called to do this. One step at a time, the process unfolded. I organized a team to conduct a feasibility study to determine whether a preschool was needed in our small community. Once we decided to proceed with opening it, one of the other team members and I were selected to co-direct the preschool. I discovered if you follow a Divine plan, there is no doubt it will manifest in Divine timing. All I had to do was hold the vision and trust the process.

After 20 wonderful years of living out my heart's passion, touching well over 1,000 little (and big) lives, I felt the nudge to move on. The times were changing, and these beautiful children were beginning to be sucked into the public-school systems. It broke my heart. These young preschoolers would go from a small, nurturing environment where they were showered with God's love, to a large classroom where hugging a child is frowned upon and the concept of God is forbidden. Not to mention, they would be bussed to school with the school-age children and their school day would be extended. As I sat contemplating in nature, grief was overwhelming. I allowed the emotion to be there. I kept asking myself, *But what about the children and their needs? Who is going to hug them and nurture them in a public school?* I knew in my heart one day there would be a change back to keeping those preschool babies at home with their parents. Who knew it would take something as big as COVID-19 to bring it to fruition, even if temporary? Who knew I was going to be placed on a new path?

It didn't take long for another vision to begin to manifest. I was led to Wisconsin Institute of Natural Wellness and began my massage career. I was introduced to various holistic healing modalities as part of the curriculum. It was in my business class when the next inspiration struck. I wasn't drawn to work in a spa. I saw myself working in a setting that included a variety of services, each operating as its own business. I envisioned a holistic healing center. I spent my transition year from the preschool actively looking for the perfect location. After ten months, I was beginning to worry. My job was ending and I didn't have anything in line to replace it.

One morning, during my prayer/meditation time, I gave up. I totally surrendered as I sarcastically told God, "Alright. You haven't opened anything up for me, so I give up! If you really want me to do this, *YOU* have to show me the place!" That morning, a former preschool parent came to me with a flyer for a yoga class. It was being offered at the school next door. I welcomed the opportunity to start working on my yoga practice and signed up immediately.

Divine timing always amazes me in hind-sight. However, for me, when I'm in the middle of trying to figure things out (ego/mind), I fail to allow the universe to do its thing (Divine flow). As it turned out, the yoga class instructor knew of a place that would welcome my business. Over the next ten years, she and I would offer our businesses in that very location.

In 2017, I began feeling the nudge to let go of the place that housed my business, Healing Grace. At least by this point, I had the understanding of divine timing and knew when the time, place, or circumstance was right, I would clearly know the way. It didn't stop me from falling into the ego-trap (as Dr. Wayne Dyer says: Edging God Out). I found myself becoming physically ill when I was wrapped up in my ego-trap. But at least I had enough experience to catch myself.

Plus, I had the beautiful practice of using the essences to guide me. This is the message Artemisia Titepati had for me:

When the information is coming too fast for you to assimilate, you may become ill. There is no need to be concerned about timing as it is all unfolding exactly as it needs to. Remember linear time and Divine time are two completely different things. There is no need to figure it out. It just is.

I was clearly reminded of this once again in early 2019, almost two years later. This time, I knew without a doubt I was to give my notice and I was to leave the center where I rented space for my work. At the same time, my siblings and I were dealing with our father's declining health. Sleep eluded me and just the thought of trying to figure out my future plans was daunting. Artemisia came to me once again with a clear reminder:

When you are receiving downloads from Source at a rate faster than you can handle, you may find your sleep becomes disrupted. You do not need to go into the three-dimensional processing mode. Just allow the messages to come and know you are retaining all that you need to retain. You are doing good as you have continued to become intentionally aware. You and those you serve have benefitted from this. Hold your vision. You do not need to figure it out. There is an invisible force working on it. It will come with Divine timing. Every encounter is preparing you for this. There is no need for you to try to figure it out. The Universe knows all of the details and all you need to do is trust the Universe.

It was reassuring to know I didn't need to be the one figuring out the next steps for any part of my life. Once again, I was reminded

God is in control. He (or She) has got this. All I needed to do was live one day at a time, one moment at a time.

I can't help but think that most people experience something similar. Have you found yourself in the whirlwind of thoughts as you try to figure out the next best step? Has this process brought you sleepless nights?

Perhaps, you, too, are receiving spiritual downloads that aren't ready to come to the surface. Be gentle with yourself. Ask the Universe to slow it down a bit or at least give you the space to sleep. Trust me. This will play an important role in your physical health and well-being.

The Path Unfolds

It has been over a year now since I received clarity on where I needed to offer my practice. The inspiration came *after* I set the date for letting go of the location I occupied. Of course! I had to release the energy of that place in order for me to open up to the energy of a new place. It all seemed so simple once the decision was made, but it took me two years to let go. Hyssop, the deva of forgiveness, blessed me with an affirming message:

Trust the place is being prepared for you. Follow the cries placed before you and you will know whether you are on the right path. Trust in the power of your healing gifts and those who have offered you healing. All are on your path for a reason. Relax and enjoy each day and each experience within your day. Layers will continue to surface and release, some of which you may not be aware, believe those experiences are Divinely guided as well. Be in a state of love at all times!

I had layers of healing that needed to happen before I could clearly see the next direction. I had lingering layers of self-doubt, forgiveness, and trust I had to work through. Questions filled my mind: Will my clients follow me if I move my business ten miles away? Will I be able to survive if I lose clients? Do I really have enough connections to build my clientele? Can I do this alone? I needed to find courage, confidence, and own my authenticity before I was ready to move on.

Perhaps you have been struggling with letting go of someone, some place, or some situation. Look for the healing gems within the struggle.

Are you able to fall into the arms of Divine timing and trust that the universe unfolds exactly as it needs to?

Which beautiful essence is calling to be used?

What messages are there for you to uncover?

Affirmations Along the Way

Step by step, I was led through that tumultuous time of transition. There is no possible way I could have known ahead of time what to do next. The path unfolded at precisely the right time, Divine time.

After my father's passing, I received a rental agreement contract for the room my business occupied. The accompanying request asked for it to be signed within the next two weeks. Two things were unsettling. First, I had only had a rental contract the first year I was there. This was a very laid-back kind of organization, which suited me just fine. Needless to say, the universe was bringing my decision front and center! Second, this was two months ahead of *MY* schedule. Now what? I was being called to stand in my authenticity with confidence. I courageously approached our director and requested an extension, which was granted. Once she agreed, I informed her that I would not be renewing my contract at the end of the two months.

My path forward was now clear. I knew without a doubt I was to move my practice home. All it needed was a little preparation and revamping. Once I realized the location was under my nose all along, I chuckled. I had been ruminating for two years over something that seemed like such a silly thing at this point. Somehow, I knew the time wouldn't have been right prior to this, but now it was. Divine timing is so amazing when we let go and let the Universe unfold. Black Pepper was the essential oil I used to support me through this process:

This is a very important time in your life right now. Your creative juices are flowing, and you are ready to take the next step. Follow your heart and be bold. Intentional awareness is your guide. Know you are fully supported and you will not fail! When you stay in the flow of creating, everything will be effortless. It is when your mind switches to the "how's" and "what if's" that the creative energy gets blocked. Remember those lower energies are sludge blocking the Universal energy from flowing. This is an exciting time for you. Embrace every moment with joy!

I had been blocking the flow of creativity by trying to bring to fruition the perfect location for my practice. I wanted to be free from the cumbersome dramas of poor maintenance and the lack of consistent custodial services. I longed to move away from the lower energy of competition. I needed my resources available and to have office space in addition to my treatment space. I had been resenting the amount of time I spent on the road commuting. And my home provided me with the perfect location. As soon as I made the decision, there was a palpable shift in my energy.

Once the floodgates were opened, the creative, strong, artistic energy continued to flow throughout the following months. I needed the time I saved by moving my practice home to allow time and space for writing. I needed to be in a place where I could create and infuse uplifting energy. I needed a space that was uniquely mine, unencumbered by others. I needed to claim my authenticity with confidence and find the courage to let go of all lower vibrations holding me back.

This is an important time in your life as well. How do I know? Simply look around at all that is going on throughout the world. We are all being called to action in one form or another. What creative energy is bubbling up within you? What synchronicity is unfolding before your eyes? What are the limiting thoughts preventing you from feeling that you are in the flow of Divine timing? Take time to ponder. Write. Sit. Listen. Remember nature is always there for you. Make space in your life to simply be present. You will be amazed at what unfolds!

"Let the beauty of what you love, be what you do. There are a thousand ways to kneel and kiss the earth." Rumi (Rumi, 2020)

Meditation

Unlimited Possibilities

As we move our attention to the top of our head, our intention is to heal, restore and align our Crown Chakra. This chakra is our connection to universal intelligence, our highest Source. When we access and clear this chakra, we are able to awaken to possibilities and receive guidance. It is powerful to realize we are not alone and we can ask for help through connection whenever we need it.

If your Crown Chakra is unbalanced, you may experience a feeling of being lost or alone. You may feel an overwhelming sense of disconnection, loneliness, or isolation. You may feel uninspired or overly concerned with material things. Or perhaps you may be drifting along aimlessly with a "head-in-the-cloud" feeling and find it difficult to take care of your physical form.

Manifestation and inspiration are born in this chakra. With an open Crown Chakra comes unlimited possibilities. Clearing and balancing your Crown Chakra and asking for help from your highest Divine guidance can bring forth awareness and answers that are beyond your wildest imagination.

Settling into a comfortable position, bring your focus to your breath. Drawing a slow, deep breath in, gently releasing with a slow, deep exhale. With each in-breath, draw your attention inward and with each out-breath release all of the cares and concerns you have carried with you to this moment. Breathing in peace, exhaling release … breathing in contentment, exhaling ease. Peace … release, contentment … ease. Peace … release, contentment … ease.

Envision a brilliant white light shining down through the top of your head. Beginning to grow, this beam of white light is fully surrounding you … Realizing you are in the center of this light … you begin to notice the white light merging with the petals of an enormous thousand-petal lotus flower … of which you are shining like a jewel in the center, becoming one with the lotus flower and remembering you are one with all creation. Effortless guidance is streaming through you and you awaken to a knowingness that you have always been connected to Source … realizing it has been quietly guiding you throughout your life. Surrendering, you embrace this amazing energy … and you are filled with peace and trust.

Gently bring your awareness back to the space you are in. Focusing on your breath once again, begin to gently move your body, feeling the energy now coursing through every fiber of your being, filling you with confidence and inspiration. Experience a deep sense of connectedness … deeper than you've ever felt previously.

When you are ready, open your eyes and embrace the unlimited possibilities awaiting you!

Essential Oil Message
Review from Chapter 7

Divine Timing

Artemisia, Titepati

When the information is coming too fast for you to assimilate, you may become ill. There is no need to be concerned about timing as it is all unfolding exactly as it needs to. Remember linear time and Divine time are two completely different things. There is no need to figure it out. It just is.

When you are receiving downloads from Source at a rate faster than you can handle, you may find your sleep becomes disrupted. You do not need to go into the three-dimensional processing mode. Just allow the messages to come and know you are retaining all that you need to retain. You are doing good as you have continued to become intentionally aware. You and those you serve have benefitted from this. Hold your vision. You do not need to figure it out. There is an invisible force working on it. It will come with Divine timing. Every encounter is preparing you for this. There is no need for you to try to figure it out. The Universe knows all of the details and all you need to do is trust the Universe.

Hyssop

Trust the place is being prepared for you. Follow the cries placed before you and you will know whether you are on the right path. Trust in the power of your healing gifts and those who have offered you healing. All are on your path for a reason. Relax and enjoy each day and each experience within your day. Layers will continue to surface and release, some of which you may not be aware, believe those experiences are Divinely guided as well. Be in a state of love at all times!

Black Pepper

This is a very important time in your life right now. Your creative juices are flowing, and you are ready to take the next step. Follow your heart and be bold. Intentional awareness is your guide. Know you are fully supported and you will not fail! When you stay in the flow of creating, everything will be effortless. It is when your mind switches to the "how's" and "what if's" that the creative energy gets blocked. Remember those lower energies are sludge blocking the Universal energy from flowing. This is an exciting time for you. Embrace every moment with joy!

Chapter 8

Encouragement

*"I only went out for a walk, and finally concluded to stay out
till sundown, for going out, I found, was really going in."*
John Muir (Wolfe, 1979)

Grandma Nan

In January 2019, I was meditating and journaling and began as I
usually do with an essence. This day, I was drawn to Ravintsara,
which is one of the essential oils who brings me encouragement. As I
inhaled her beautiful scent, I was drawn to a picture on my altar of my
Grandma Nan. She was my mother's mother who died giving birth to
my mom. My mom blessed me with her name. This provided a way
for her to carry on the memory of her mother. When I became an adult,
my mom gifted me a few of her mother's items. One of them was a
tiny birthday book that has a few entries written in my grandmother's

handwriting, and one was a picture of my Grandma Nan. I treasure those pieces of my history.

This particular morning, I felt the nudge to pick up her picture as she beckoned me to gaze into her eyes. I clearly heard her speaking to me as if she were sitting right next to me:

You are me. That is why your mom was drawn to name you after me and why you felt drawn to be called Grandma Nan by your grandchildren. You embody my temperament ... your edginess, quick temper, and impatience all come from me. The messages you bring to others and the urgency of those messages are why you have a short fuse. Your ultimate desire is for all beings to evolve and heal at the same time you are healing. You are impatient with the materialistic world you occupy. I, too, felt the same way, but I was born at a time when the world wasn't ready. It is why I left earth so young. Your courage to step out and be different comes from your Grandma Pauline [my dad's mom]. Draw on her for support when courage is needed. Be at peace with who you are and embrace all of your emotions. Go deep within to discover their roots. You will see the connection between your passion and perceived obstacles. Know these obstacles are there to strengthen you and embrace them. This is a year for you to be bold. Step out and do not fear! You ARE a magnificent sovereign being of Divine love and light!

This whole business of being a "listener" is fairly new to me. But as these messages are channeled through to me, I have no doubt they are authentic and true. This particular message left me feeling humbled, filled with gratitude, and blessed to be receiving this truly amazing gift.

Two weeks later, I was called to use the unique essential oil Curcuma Zedoaria. I asked for guidance and to be open to what needed to be revealed and once again, Grandma Nan was clearly present within. She affirmed that my mom was present as well. Her clear message was:

Sacred Contracts. Yes, there is something in there you need to read. You will be led. Trust.

I obediently went to my bookcase and pulled Sacred Contracts by Carolyn Myss (Myss, 2001) off my shelf. I didn't remember ever completely reading it, and I began to peruse the pages. I was drawn first to the section on chakras and then somehow landed on page 72: *"... our own flaws serve to conceal the valuable nature of our potential contribution to humanity...we still tend to focus more on our faults than on our capacities and promise. And yet, we all hold within us the potential for greatness and the potential to be of great service to others."* This was exactly the message Grandma Nan delivered two weeks prior. "Intentional Awareness" was my theme for 2019, and I could clearly see this was going to be an incredible year.

I suggest trying this yourself. Bring to mind one of your ancestors. If you are able, find a picture of the person you choose. Gaze into their eyes.

Are you aware of any of their qualities that mirror qualities within yourself?

What might this be saying to you about your path?

Does this provide you with insight into your own healing journey?

Stand in Your Truth

There are many great books available to help those who want to heal from past wounds. I recently worked through the book Growing the Positive Mind by William K. Larkin (Larkin, 2016). I'm sure I was led to this book primarily because I was caught in a vicious cycle of judgment, being critical (judgmental!) of others for their judgmental-ness, being critical of situations that led to judgment. I wanted to escape from that cycle. As I've said, I now realize this is a work in progress. It was interesting how this book crossed my path at the time I was ready to receive it. I had purchased it for one of the yoga trainings I had gone through but I hadn't taken the time to read it. As I was preparing for a trip, I wanted an engaging book to read. I walked over to one of my shelves and started reviewing what I had. I don't know how it happened, other than through Divine intervention, but this book literally fell off of the shelf in front of me. I was intrigued by the title and realized it was serendipitous!

William Larkin's book helped me understand what lower vibrations were keeping me in what he calls a downward spiral, so I set the intention to work toward the emotions that kept me in an upward spiral. Part of this work involved embracing my strengths. I took an online timed test (CliftonStrengths) which identified my top five strengths: Intellection, Connectedness, Learner, Empathy, and Developer. All of these fit and made perfect sense. The unfolding of all I learned from Larkin's book prepared me to be in a place of readiness to complete the book you are reading.

The first thing I am called to do when I have a life-changing revelation is to share it. I want everyone to be given the same opportunities I have been given. This totally fits with my strengths as it involves putting all into action. As I sat meditating with Fir Balsam, she brought me a strong message:

All of nature is here to support you as you stand strong. You are ready to go out. You have the tools in place. You have been clearing and continue to clear the debris blocking your progression. Encourage others to meditate and listen to nature. See yourself teaching, connecting, and encouraging others. Your path is unfolding before you. When you introduce yourself, say: 'I am a magnificent sovereign being of Divine love, and SO ARE YOU'. As you look each one in the eyes, pause and let it sink in. Continue by saying: 'I have a passion to share what I have learned along my soul's journey, what I have found to be Truth within me. Some of what I share may resonate with you and some may not. I come to you with unconditional love in my heart for each of you, and I speak my Truth from my heart'. It is important to start each of your teachings this way as not everyone is ready to absorb what you have to say. You are being led and opportunities are unfolding. Remember, you are supported as you stand in your Truth.

Is Spirit talking to you as well?

Are you being encouraged to step out boldly?

Are you able to confidently speak your Truth, even if others may not be ready to hear what you have to say?

Let this message be your reminder. You, too, are being guided. You, too, are a magnificent sovereign being of Divine love.

Courage and Confidence

Throughout my years I have followed Divine timing, however, I find myself slipping into phases of doubt. This usually unfolds as I experience the uneasy feeling of something new on the horizon, but I'm not quite sure what it is going to be. It almost feels like once I get comfortable with my life, something starts to stir within me. My typical response is to question my calling. Sometimes this happens out of the blue, and sometimes circumstances around me trigger this response.

Four years after I had established my massage business, I had become quite comfortable with my schedule and my practice was slowly building. I was confident I was on the right path; I enjoyed my clients and I looked forward to each day. That is, until my husband was forced into an early retirement. His response was for me to find a full-time job with benefits to support us through this transition. This was a very challenging decision for me. I trusted the path I was on was the right path, and it felt great to be a part of helping others along their healing journey. Did I need to give up everything I had established and follow a different path?

I meditated. I prayed. I listened to my Higher Guidance. Not one time did I hear I needed to give up my new practice. I was clearly on the right path. Almost daily, I double-checked to make sure I was correctly hearing the guidance of the Universe. Would God make my path so clear and then in the blink of an eye change it? I kept hearing, "Stay on the course. Trust and believe." And so, I did. It took several years before my husband was able to find his career groove again. We made it through, and I was able to continue along the path I was meant to be on.

This pattern of doubt, wondering whether I'm on the right path, rattles within me. I need to clarify here. I do know I've been on the right path; however, I periodically get the feeling there is more I need to be doing. I've learned to sit with it and meditate. I find I simply need to ask the Universe "Is there more I should be doing?" One particular time, Rosewood helped channel this message to me:

Stay strong in your faith and have courage to continue on the path of helping others raise their vibration. When doubts or obstacles get in your way, turn to us as we are always here to assist as you move forward. Always live from the place of the upward spiral. Remember, we are a catalyst in helping humans heal on all levels. Many are ready for this type of ascending movement, and we are excited to help all on their journey. Just as we have been helping you!

I continued to wonder whether I needed to do more:

Do your own work and make this a priority. As you do your own work, revelations and experiences will provide you with pertinent information to share.

As I was pondering this inspirational message, I was reminded of dreams I recently had and the connections I had been making with others in the spirit world. All of those experiences brought me a sense of joy and excitement. I was also prompted to incorporate music into my life and my teachings as music heals and connects the soul. It is through very simple practices that we can receive affirmations and guidance.

If courage is something you seek in your life, try asking yourself the following questions.

What is holding you back from moving forward with your inner calling?

Do you have clarity on what path you need to be on? If not, why not? If so, what is holding you back?

What would it take to bring courage forth to help you proceed?

What ways do you find encouragement to follow your inner guidance?

Are you taking the time necessary to do your own healing work?

Loneliness Journey

As a child and teen, my family spent our summers at a campground about 40 minutes from our home. My dad commuted to work each day and every evening my parents enjoyed the respite from the busyness of city life. My brother and I had all the luxuries a child could want--playground, lake, game room, friends.

I was a very contemplative child. Some called me a day-dreamer, not in a positive way. I loved being in nature. For me, lying on the hillside overlooking the lake brought me great peace and joy. My parents thought I was a recluse and needed to be more active. My brother couldn't sit still long enough to even begin to be a part of my world. I remember having a deep longing, wanting to share the experience with someone, but no one seemed interested. Even star-gazing at night on the hill was something I had to enjoy alone.

This feeling of loneliness has followed me most of my life, especially when I began to shed all of the people, places, and things in my life that didn't align with my inner Truth. As I moved through my healing experiences, I found, once again, I had no one who could move through them with me. I had a yearning for a soulmate or friend to share my journey and the exciting discoveries I'd had with nature, healing, and spirituality. I yearned for someone in my life to be on the same page. This feeling of loneliness was haunting me one morning. Just when I needed her message, the beautiful, sun-kissed essence of Goldenrod shone through for me:

Get out in nature and you will find your soul connection. This is where your creativity will flow. This is what you are missing living in a climate that keeps you trapped inside through the long months of winter. You must get outside, no matter what. Find peace within, and you can be your own soulmate.

On cold or rainy days, I have to force myself to get out into nature. Once out there, I find solace and peace and the soul connection I long for, even when I am alone. As humans, we often look for someone to validate us or in the very least, talk through our musings. We are never alone, even if physically there is no one around us. Nature is God's way of manifesting love in a physical form. All we need to do is pause, see the beauty, and feel the unconditional love of our Creator, tuning out the noise of our minds and finding our true soulmate, who is always within us.

It took many years for me to label the experience I was having as loneliness.

Do you tend to seek encouragement from outside of you, or are you content finding it within?

What words of encouragement are you longing to hear?

Can you whisper them to yourself?

Take a moment to pause, breathe deeply, and tap into your inner soulmate!

Meditation

Releasing Fear

Our Root Chakra is located at the base of our spine in the region of the Coccyx. Also known as the Base Chakra, it is where our sense of being grounded and feeling secure originates. It is our connection to Mother Earth. This sense of being grounded is essential for living a conscious life and making choices for our highest good. When we are grounded, we are present and able to be aware of the people in our life as well as our surroundings.

We know if this chakra is imbalanced when fear is at the core of our daily lives, preventing us from moving through an experience or taking the first step to move forward: fear of the unknown, fear of failure, fear of what others' perception of us might be, fear that we aren't _____ enough, fear that we don't have enough, fear of change.

To be at a place in our lives where we feel balanced and alive, it is imperative that we release our fears, replacing fear with courage … strength … stability … truth … trust … hope.

Preparing for our meditation journey, begin by taking in a few slow deep breaths, drawing your breath deep, down into the diaphragm. Slowly releasing the exhale, allow the diaphragm to release. Focus only on your slow deep breaths. Release any thoughts or concerns as you bring your awareness to this present moment of time. Exhale and relax more and more as you become totally present with your life-giving breath.

Bring your awareness to your Root Chakra, imagine you are a seed. You are planted, nourished and given all you need to grow and survive. Envision, like a tree, your roots are tethering you to our beautiful Mother Earth while connecting you to your Creator or Source. Feel the energy moving freely throughout your being and see this energy as a beautiful, deep shade of red surrounding and protecting you. You are safe. You are nurtured. You are connected. Your divine connection to Source brings you exactly what you need at all times and in all places. Bask in the warm glow of this beautiful energy, know you are completely whole… content as you have all you need to survive and thrive as you've been created to do.

The red energy is enveloping you and protecting you. As you carry this sense of being protected and supported, ask yourself … What fear is presenting itself to me at this moment? Allow time for Source to bring it to your awareness. Notice any changes in your breath … or changes in your physical body's ability to relax. When you are clear about the fear, surround it with your beautiful red energy and replace your fear with courage, strength, stability, truth, trust, hope. Feel a sense of unwavering certainty that all is well … you are completely protected and guided. Trust the gifts the universe is offering you. Embrace them with confidence!

Slowly bring your awareness back to your natural breath, moving your body, opening your eyes. Engulfed in a sense of belonging and grounded-ness, feel encouraged to move forward.

Essential Oil Message
Review from Chapter 8

Encouragement

Fir Balsam

All of nature is here to support you as you stand strong. You are ready to go out. You have the tools in place. You have been clearing and continue to clear the debris blocking your progression. Encourage others to meditate and listen to nature. See yourself teaching, connecting, and encouraging others. Your path is unfolding before you. When you introduce yourself, say: 'I am a magnificent sovereign being of Divine love, and SO ARE YOU'. As you look each one in the eyes, pause and let it sink in. Continue by saying: 'I have a passion to share what I have learned along my soul's journey, what I have found to be Truth within me. Some of what I share may resonate with you and some may not. I come to you with unconditional love in my heart for each of you, and I speak my Truth from my heart'. It is important to start each of your teachings this way as not everyone is ready to absorb what you have to say. You are being led and opportunities are unfolding. Remember, you are supported as you stand in your Truth.

Rosewood

Stay strong in your faith and have courage to continue on the path of helping others raise their vibration. When doubts or obstacles get in your way, turn to us as we are always here to assist as you move forward. Always live from the place of the upward spiral. Remember, we are a catalyst in helping humans heal on all levels. Many are ready for this type of ascending movement, and we are excited to help all on their journey. Just as we have been helping you!

Do your own work and make this a priority. As you do your own work, revelations and experiences will provide you with pertinent information to share.

Goldenrod

Get out in nature and you will find your soul connection. This is where your creativity will flow. This is what you are missing living in a climate that keeps you trapped inside through the long months of winter. You must get outside, no matter what. Find peace within, and you can be your own soulmate.

Gratitude

So much to be thankful for

Gifts bigger than we can fathom

The sky

Water

Fresh air

The sun

Human connections, animal connections

Family and friends

Colors so vivid

Green growing things

People caring for people

Music and the sounds of nature

Tastes of so many varieties

Our breath, our life

Our Creator, our God

-2015

Chapter 9

Gratitude

"Give thanks in all circumstances" *1 Thessalonians 5:18*

Mindful Gratitude Practice

I have adopted a more mindful gratitude practice over the past decade. I always thought of myself as a grateful person. However, once I began an intentional practice, I realized how much of my life I took for granted.

Simply being grateful for a new day to live life to the fullest is a great way to start the day. If it is raining, I give thanks for the ground being replenished. If it is sunny and warm, I find myself outside giving thanks for the warmth and nourishment of the sun. If I wake up to snow, even after a long winter, I give thanks for the beauty and purity of the white blanket. I thank God for my family, my friends, my clients, and anyone else who comes to mind. When I do this, my day is off to a good start. If I forget to do this simple practice, my whole day unfolds differently. I become more inward focused, not in a healthy way but instead focusing on my physical aches and pains. This quickly turns into worries and, I have to admit, then grumpiness creeps in. It amazes me how the mind can respond so differently to these practices.

I also end my day with a gratitude practice. As I lay my head on my pillow, I begin to recall all of the blessings that came my way. I usually drift off into a peaceful sleep. If I awaken during the middle of the night, I continue with my gratitude practice. Here again, if I forget this practice, sleep seems to be more disturbed.

Several years ago, while reading Growing the Positive Mind by William Larkin (Larkin, 2016), I chose to deepen my practice. In his book, Mr. Larkin suggests you pulse each of the higher vibrational emotions of love, joy, peace, hope, and gratitude. This practice is designed to help you notice how your body feels when you are con-necting with a particular emotion. He suggests you stop and notice what changes occur within your body. To further your practice, he also suggests you find a song to correlate with the emotion. For gratitude, I searched YouTube and found a great song entitled "Grateful" by Nimo Patel (Patel, 2013). It became my go-to song whenever I needed a gratitude attitude adjustment. I also chose one of my beloved essential oils, Marjoram. Here is the message Marjoram brought forth:

As gratitude fills your heart, it will make room for uncon-ditional love to be at the forefront. Marjoram will help you release unnecessary energies that may prevent you from truly experiencing a heart of gratitude.

This practice of gratitude has been instrumental in clearing out my old patterns of jealousy, judgment, worry, fear, and resentment … just to name a few. Larkin also recommends making a list of 50 things you are grateful for. I use this practice at the beginning of each year to help me stay focused on all of the blessings and gifts present in my life. Throughout the year, if I am having an "off" day, I will go back to my list and recall my bountiful blessings.

I encourage you to begin your own gratitude practice if you don't already have one. It is great to have the visual list, too. Take the time to write a list of 50 things you are grateful for in your life right now, even if you are in a slump and can't seem to think of anything. One of my students claimed she couldn't think of 50 things she was grateful for, so I encouraged her to think about each one of her body parts as individuals to be thanked. For instance, be thankful for your mouth for giving you the opportunity to talk and eat, for your feet that hold you up when you stand, for your eyes that see your surroundings, etc. There is much we take for granted. Just recognizing and being grateful for our bodies could fill a page! Enjoy the process. I am grateful for you. I am also grateful you are taking the time to read this and develop your own gratitude practice.

Gratitude Expands the Heart

"The more grateful we are, the more connected
we become in the universe around us."
Stephen Richards (Richards, 2020)

Twenty years ago, one of my sons moved out East to go to school. He and his partner eventually moved out of New York City and into a nearby city in Connecticut. Throughout his years in NYC, he mostly worked retail and therefore wasn't able to travel home for the holidays. Being the traditionalist I am, this was difficult for me. Once his partner came into the picture, I was told they had family traditions for the holidays that couldn't be broken. Evidently there were expectations they had to meet that included events at each of his divorced parents' homes. The seed of jealousy was planted.

It didn't take too long before my son and his partner began to travel the world with the in-laws. This fueled the growth of my jealousy. I was on an inward crash course, with jealousy morphing to include a barrage of other negative emotions as I berated myself for feeling jealous rather than being happy for them. I wanted to be happy for them. I even told them I was happy for them. But I just couldn't feel it inside. My mind was spiraling downward with jealousy, guilt, and shame, and I felt out of control.

All of this began to shift as I deepened my gratitude practice. Little by little, I was able to feel joy for my son. He had such a loving family who welcomed him into their fold. Marjoram was there to assist me through the process:

As you continue to feel gratitude in your heart, unconditional love will grow. Take time this week as your heart opens and prepares you for your work. Live from this place of gratitude and love. Be the example to others. Observing is not judging. Be diligent about knowing and understanding the difference. Each time you encounter a person who you believe isn't on a path of awakening, send that person unconditional love. Shine your light even brighter. They are in your life for a reason. Let your path unfold and enjoy the journey!

I gave myself space to meditate on all I held in gratitude. This led me to release the lower energy of jealousy. I became grateful that my son has another "mom" who lives closer to him and is there for him whenever he needs her. Those years of struggling with envy were quickly melting away. Jealousy had been replaced by deep gratitude and unconditional love. I was able to see her kindness, generosity, and love for him as genuine, and I felt so blessed she was in his life.

Gratitude may be something you take for granted, as I did. Allow these prompts to take you deeper into your practice.

What situations or people in your life are bringing emotions to the surface for you?

Is it possible to see them in a different way…one of gratitude?

Try it. Through a new lens, you, too, may find unconditional love and gratitude.

Gratitude: Bringer of Hope

As I write this, our world is in the middle of a pandemic, and our economy is suffering with unemployment at the highest it has been for decades. Not only is our country divided on how we should move through this challenging time, but peaceful protests have turned violent over the wrongful, unnecessary deaths of George Floyd and other people of color. I'm sickened by the injustices of humankind. At times like this, I'm saddened to be part of the human race. I'm perplexed by the insensitivities of so many people. The unprecedented millennial shift is upon us. Who knew this shift would be felt so deeply?

Because I am a highly sensitive person, I find myself feeling these shifts physically, emotionally and spiritually. I am grateful I have a spiritual practice that keeps me centered and grounded. During times like this, I know I must turn back to my gratitude practices in order to find the strength and hope to move forward in life. Without these practices, I would be curled up under a blanket waiting for the world to end. When helplessness and hopelessness creep in, I turn to one of my favorite prayers, the prayer of St. Francis:

Make me a channel of Your peace;
Where there is hatred, let me sow love;

Where there is injury, pardon;

Where there is doubt, faith;

Where there is despair, hope;

Where there is darkness, light;

And where there is sadness, joy.

It is my personal prayer that we all find the inner strength to move forward with grace, gratitude, and hope in the days and weeks ahead, and that this world may come to a place where peace and harmony prevail. Here is a passage from the Holy Bible that helps strengthen my spiritual resiliency through turbulent times: *"Now faith is being sure of what we hope for and certain of what we do not see." Hebrews 11:1 (NRSV)* I turned to the pungent essence of Mugwort to bring this message forth:

I bring you hope. Hope differs from wishing. Hope reminds you that all things are possible with the help of the Holy Spirit. Hope for peace in the world. Hope for all opportunities to manifest for your family and friends. Hope for all humanity to discover their inner Light. Hope for equality among all peoples.

Spend time taking in the prayer of St. Francis. Are you ready to be a channel of peace? Take a moment to mindfully hold the whole world in the palm of your hand. Repeat the prayer. Then, turn to your gratitude list and reread it. Use this practice to raise your vibrations and restore and ground yourself.

Growth Through Gratitude

For the past seven years, I have had the blessed privilege of leading a week-long women's retreat in Andros, Bahamas. This was another one of those inspirations that came through and I had no idea how it was going to manifest. I held the vision for a number of years, and then one day, out of the blue, I was given the name and phone number of a woman who lived near me in Wisconsin and owned a home in Andros, Bahamas. Trusting this coincidence was Divinely orchestrated, I reached out and we became partners for these retreats. I was inspired to gather women away from their daily lives, introduce them to an unfamiliar culture, and provide them with a venue and theme to guide their healing journey.

I spend many hours preparing for the seven days we are together. What I didn't plan for was my own healing to unfold, which occurred on various levels. Healing surfaced for me through the encounters and dealings with the retreaters, collaboration with other people, trusting the Universe to bring exactly who needed to be present, and having faith that my financial obligations were met. The big realization came through the recognition of the silent judge within me.

Being immersed in another culture sheds light on our silent prejudices. Who says our culture has the right views on life? Who says our moral standards are the correct moral standards? Where did the seeds of division between those who "have" and those who "have not" originate? It is as simple as looking at a foreign country and thinking, "Why do they drive on the 'wrong' side of the road?"

The Androsians are some of the happiest, most content people I have met. On a tourist brochure I picked up years ago the caption reads: Andros, La Isla d'Espirito Santo (the Island of the Holy Spirit). Indeed, it is a holy place of healing.

Each year, I come away from the retreat with new insights into healing old layers and old patterns. I welcome them and honor them for the blessed gift they bring. Rosemary Verbenone brought me the following message one year as I was preparing for the retreat. I had fallen into the lower energy of worry:

Set the intention of what you want to accomplish and stay with it. As humans, you do this but then you continue to worry. In other words, you think you are in control or are not doing enough. It all comes down to trust--complete trust that all will unfold exactly as it should. Your earthly "needs" are met in other ways. You see it but don't fully find gratitude. Your worthiness is not based on monetary income. You know this but have yet to embrace it in your heart. All you can do is trust and believe and live from a place of gratitude. Deep gratitude. You have come a long way. Yes, layers have been released. You are ready, my Beloved, to move deeper into your heart. You are a magnificent sovereign being of Divine love! You are loved and supported always!

Of course! Deep gratitude is the key. Sit in gratitude and trust whatever new lessons appear will bring me deeper into my heart. Part of my work in Andros includes offering my healing touch to the local people, mostly women. These strong, beautiful women continually give to their families and their community, often neglecting themselves. There is a law in the Bahamas stating foreigners cannot earn wages. At first, I was cautious as I didn't want to spend my whole time-off offering free massages. But each gift I offered brought more to me than I could have imagined. The heart-connections made were a blessed gift. Indeed, I've come a long way, but I know I will continue to heal layers within myself regardless of where I am on this Earth.

Healing comes in many ways through people, situations, and encounters we have every day of our lives. What areas in your life need a new perspective? Find the pearls to be thankful for and increase your practice of gratitude. Instead of berating yourself, be thankful for the opportunities presenting themselves. Practice gratitude on a daily basis, and you will find your heart expanding. Enjoy the process. I am grateful for you. I am also grateful you are taking the time to read this and develop your own gratitude practice.

"I thank you God for this most amazing day, for the leaping greenly spirits of trees, and for the blue dream of sky and for everything which is natural, which is infinite, which is yes." e. e. cummings (cummings, 2020)

Meditation

A Grateful Heart

Find a comfortable position and begin this practice by focusing on your breath. As you continue to slow your breath rate, bring your awareness to your feet. Sense your toes. With your next breath relax each toe a little bit more ... your big toe, second toe, and so on. Imagine what life would be like without your toes. Give thanks for their presence and support. Notice how they are connected to your foot. Bring your awareness to your whole foot ... your sole, your arch, your heel, all of them together. Give thanks for the support of your feet, honoring them by giving them a little massage.

Work your way up to your ankles and then your calves, your knees and your thighs. With each breath relax any given part as you focus on it. Give thanks for them as they work together to form your legs. Gently honor them by massaging or rubbing each one as you recognize the gift they are in your life ... holding you up, moving you forward ... walking, running, cycling.

Continue your body scan, move up to your hips and your pelvis. Using your breath, relax any tension present and move in a way that helps release any discomfort from this area of your body. Imagine what limitations would present themselves if you didn't have fully functioning hips and pelvis. Give thanks for the presence and functions of this area of your body.

Work your way up your spine, envision each vertebra stacked upon another. Slowly release any tension along your spine from the base up to where it meets your skull. Mindfully move your spine in ways that will allow any tension to melt away. Give thanks for the flexibility of your spine, the movement and strength it provides for your mobility and stability. Bring your awareness to the front of your body, gently massaging your tummy area, your sides, your chest … release any tension in the front side. Give thanks for all occupants of this area of your body … internal and external.

Continue up the body to your shoulders and neck, move these areas in a mindful way to release any tension residing here. Give thanks for burdens the shoulders have carried. Give thanks for the neck connecting your head to your torso.

Focus on your head, begin by bringing your awareness to your jaw. Release your jaw. Notice your ears. Release tension in and around your ears. Notice your scalp and hair. Gently grasp your hair and pull, release tension in the scalp or gently massage the scalp, feel the tension resolve. Give thanks for your jaw, scalp, and hair.

Draw your attention to your face. Soften the muscles around your eyes, your cheeks, your nose, your mouth. Cover your face softly with your hands. Feel the warmth comforting you. Lightly massage your face, release any tension. Give thanks for all that your eyes have allowed you to see, for your nose and the wonderful smells it has brought you and for the opportunity to breathe, for your mouth and its ability to nourish your body and for giving you the gift of speech.

Place your hands over your heart. Allow a deep sense of gratitude to emerge. Honoring your body for all of its gifts in this way will open your heart to see all life through the lens of gratitude. Take as long as you need and then slowly open your eyes.

Essential Oil Message
Review from Chapter 9

Gratitude

Marjoram

As gratitude fills your heart, it will make room for unconditional love to be at the forefront. Marjoram will help you release unnecessary energies that may prevent you from truly experiencing a heart of gratitude.

As you continue to feel gratitude in your heart, unconditional love will grow. Take time this week as your heart opens and prepares you for your work. Live from this place of gratitude and love. Be the example to others. Observing is not judging. Be diligent about knowing and understanding the difference. Each time you encounter a person who you believe isn't on a path of awakening, send that person unconditional love. Shine your light even brighter. They are in your life for a reason. Let your path unfold and enjoy the journey!

Mugwort

I bring you hope. Hope differs from wishing. Hope reminds you that all things are possible with the help of the Holy Spirit. Hope for peace in the world. Hope for all opportunities to manifest for your family and friends. Hope for all humanity to discover their inner Light. Hope for equality among all peoples.

Rosemary, Verbenone

Set the intention of what you want to accomplish and stay with it. As humans, you do this but then you continue to worry. In other words, you think you are in control or are not doing enough. It all comes down to trust--complete trust that all will unfold exactly as it should. Your earthly "needs" are met in other ways. You see it but don't fully find gratitude. Your worthiness is not based on monetary income. You know this but have yet to embrace it in your heart. All you can do is trust and believe and live from a place of gratitude. Deep gratitude. You have come a long way. Yes, layers have been released. You are ready, my Beloved, to move deeper into your heart. You are a magnificent sovereign being of Divine love! You are loved and supported always!

The Depth of His Love

"I forgive you your sins."

How can this be?

It sounds so simple …

But is it for me?

I've discovered the depth

Of His love for mankind.

But is it that easy

To leave my sins behind?

His life was so pure

So blameless, you see.

Yet He's willing to suffer …

For you and for me.

"Lay your burdens at my feet,

It is what you must do.

It is why I came to Earth,

To heal others, to heal you."

-2007

131

Chapter 10

Joy, Love, and Amazing Grace

"May my soul bloom in love for all existence."
Rudolf Steiner (Steiner, 2020)

Life Without Joy

When I was in my thirties, I didn't have a clue what true joy felt like. I vaguely remembered the joy of birthing my two babies a decade or more earlier, but life felt so heavy and difficult by this point that the word joy wasn't in my vocabulary. I was living in a dysfunctional marriage, was raising two teenage boys, and friends were either moving away or involved in their own lives. I was working three jobs to fill my time, which conveniently kept me from having to be at home.

During this time, I was invited to attend a spiritual all-day workshop entitled "Words of Blessing." The woman who founded the ministry, Mary Crist, started hearing messages from Jesus shortly after her son committed suicide. It was through this amazing gift that she began these workshops. The day was filled with testimonies, meditative practices, and fellowship. We all were invited to participate in an activity that involved going to a table covered with stones of every shape, size, and color--stones that were a gift from one of the team members. When he walked along the river bank, he would pick up each stone that called to him. When he held the stone, a word would come to him and he would write it on the stone. He offered these stones for our meditative practice. As we approached the table, we were encouraged to choose the one we were drawn to. All of the words were hidden on the underside, so we were purely drawn by the characteristics of the stone itself. Once selected, we took it back to our table without turning it over. When everyone had their stone, we were given time to answer some basic questions...Why were you drawn to that particular stone? What is it trying to tell you? After we spent time reflecting on those questions, we were told to lovingly receive the word or words found on the other side of our stone and to reflect on any feelings those words elicited. My word was "joy." I sat staring at the stone completely blank as I had no connection to *that* word whatsoever in *that* moment. When I shared my reaction with one of the leaders, she encouraged me to be open to receive joy. She suggested I keep the stone as a reminder that joy *is* present in life. To this day, I have kept that stone in a special place as my reminder.

I don't want to paint a picture that I was always experiencing doom and gloom. I certainly wasn't on the outside. My astrological sign is Aries. Aries keep their lives together. We make things happen. We are driven. To the outside world, I was a high-energy leader. I was someone who would get the task done. If there was a need, I was there to fill it. I was involved in my church and whatever school my boys were in at the time. I helped with Scouting activities and was a supportive sports mom. I served on the Music Committee at their high school and was the treasurer for their musical each year. I totally devoted all of my free time to being involved in my two boys' lives. It was the only way I could cope with the failing marriage and dysfunction that permeated my life. Chin up, smile on the face. I walked through life masking the absence of joy.

At some point, I was introduced to Al-Anon. Of course, I thought I was going there to learn how I could fix the problem back home. I loved the gentle people who were part of my first Al-Anon group. They were genuinely caring, loving people and weren't afraid to call me out on my stinking thinking. I quickly learned that when I had one finger pointing at someone else (mostly my husband whom I blamed for my demise), I also had three fingers pointing back at myself. This meant I should not just focus on the direction of the one finger, but instead reflect three times more on the inward direction and question why I was justifying the finger pointing. Over time, this program saved me.

I began to see life differently. I saw where I was powerless. I let go of trying to fix the problem and instead focused on repairing myself. I'll just say that taking a fearless self-inventory IS NOT an easy thing to do, but it is a necessary tool that can bring unfathomable benefits. From that point on, brick by brick of the wall I had built around myself began to fall away. What emerged was my true self who began to embrace and see life through the eyes of joy. The essential oil Tamarack has been my faithful companion to help bring joy forth:

I bring you joy. Remember to feel joy throughout all situations...the kind of joy you feel when you are with your grandchildren or someone special to you. Joy with family. Joy with places that challenge you. Joy with winter. Joy in the beauty of nature. Always be aware of JOY!

The term *"joie de vivre"* is a French term translating to "joy of life." I had mistaken joy for happiness in the story reflected above.

Now I can see the difference. Bringing that word into my life, even though it started on a small stone, became one of the biggest changes within me. If I do not feel the *joie de vivre* in something now, I quickly move on and replace it with something that does bring me joy.

Reflect on the word "joy" for a moment. What connection do you have to it?

Can you easily relate to such a simple word?

What really brings *joie de vivre* into your life?

How do you take the time to recognize it and honor it for its presence?

Nature Expands Joy

When I think of nature, I think of being outside in the natural world. Whether it is in a garden, forest, field of clover, or sandy beach at the edge of the ocean, it doesn't matter. I feel peaceful and content. Sometimes, just sitting on my deck and being surrounded by the sights, sounds, and fresh air is all I need to regain my connection to her. This evokes a feeling of blissful satisfaction. One morning, Tamarack brought me a Divine message:

Listen with your heart. Embrace all of life's experiences with joy, not judgment. Connect with nature on a deeper level. All of nature is here to guide you, bringing beauty to the earth. Enjoy its beauty. It is true many plants and trees don't belong in certain areas. Nature brings beauty wherever it lives, even if only for a short season. Be mindful and be grateful. Then all of God's creation is happy.

In the Midwest, our pleasurable seasons are rather short. For me, the question is: How do I enjoy the beauty of nature without judgment of the temperature and lack of vibrant colors? My body does not do well with the cold of winter. I tend to hunker down indoors with multiple layers on, just to keep warm. Occasionally a bright, sunny, snowy day will beckon me out for a walk, but only if the wind is fairly calm will I venture out. Instead of judging what I don't have, I find joy in what I do have available. Connecting with nature can be as simple as talking to your plants while you water them, adding some beautiful essence to your diffuser to bring a delicious scent to the air, or simply stepping inward and communing with nature through visualization or meditation.

Reflect on your experience with joy as you unite with nature in your own special way. In what ways does it bring you joy?

What forms of nature are you drawn to?

What experiences of joy are evoked when you make the time to be present in nature?

Take a walk in a forest, stroll along the beach, paddle down a river, or perhaps brighten a room with fresh-cut flowers or flowering plants. Implement whatever is possible option for you to bring more reminders of joy into your life.

Through Grace Comes Love

I pondered "love" as I prepared to write this chapter. In my heart, I know God is a God of love, which seemingly conflicts with what I was taught in confirmation class. We were taught "You need to *fear*, love, and trust God..." with an emphasis on the word fear. Those early years planted the seed of fear: fear of making a mistake, fear of damnation when I did make a mistake, fear I would be separated from my family if I didn't obey, fear I would suffer awful consequences if I went down the wrong path. Fear made me feel separate from God because I was such an imperfect person and figured I was doomed by my imperfections.

Throughout my rebellious teen years, I did what many teenagers of the 1970's did. I escaped from the reality of my imperfections through getting high or getting drunk, and I began "looking for love in all the wrong places." My grandmother always reminded me we have an angel on one shoulder and the devil on the other. Our choices depended on which one we were listening to each moment. I existed by vacillating between oblivion and remorse for many years, always wondering what my awful consequences would be.

It was during this troubled time of my life, mid-teens, when I was date-raped. At the time, I blamed myself for drinking and for putting myself in that situation. I was 16; he was 22. Today he would be considered a sex offender. He stole my virginity and I lived with complete regret. I went through many years of turmoil because of that traumatic event. I was also taught in my faith tradition that through the body, blood, and resurrection of Christ, I was forgiven. This unconditional forgiveness was offered each time I received the Sacrament of Communion. I was forgiven for all my "sins." For many years, I saw Christ and God as two different entities. I believed Jesus forgave me, but God judged me unworthy. I lost my connection to who I truly was.

This uncertainty manifested in low self-esteem and remained within me until 2005 when I was in my late 40's. I had been dealing with tendonitis in my right elbow for almost two years. I had followed the western medicine protocol and received two shots of cortisone and a couple of physical therapy sessions. The doctor had told me if I had another flare up, I would need surgery. There was no way I wanted to undergo surgery, so when the tendonitis flared up again, I ignored it…until I could no longer hold a cup of coffee with that hand as the pain shot through my entire arm.

One day, while running errands, my attention was drawn to an acupuncture clinic. Knowing nothing about acupuncture, I stopped in to see if acupuncture could treat tendonitis. Within a few days I began my journey to healing on all levels: physical, mental, emotional, and spiritual. After several months of working through the physical issues with Craniosacral Therapy and Acupuncture, the emotional and spiritual healing finally came through. My practitioner had been encouraging me to allow the memory stuck in the tissues to surface and release. For the longest time, I stayed in my mind, trying to figure it out. She would say, "Get out of your head" over and over again. And then, out of the blue, it happened. I immediately saw myself on the hill with my right arm pinned down, and I was being raped. The emotions of shame and guilt poured out as I sobbed. In the same moment, I saw Jesus pick me up, carry me, and say, "I forgave you a long time ago. I've been waiting for you to forgive yourself." The flood gates opened and for the first time, I truly loved myself. In all of my brokenness and through all of the choices, good and not so good, I finally loved myself enough to let go of the guilt and shame I had carried for so many decades. Grace, amazing healing grace.

There is a beautiful essence that helps bring us to a place of loving ourselves. Here is the message that Violet shared with me:

I am a gentle love opener. I bring new life to you as love grows and emanates from you. I am here to calm fears, mend the broken-hearted, and heal blocks to giving and receiving love.

The tendonitis healing process was completed. Once the emotional and spiritual levels were healed, the physical followed. My desire to enter into a holistic healing career path was opened through this experience. After such a profound experience, I knew without a doubt, I somehow had to get this message out to others who harbored emotions preventing them from feeling complete self-love. Grace has been defined as unmerited favor, something each human is offered if only we accept it. To experience grace in this remarkable way was truly life-changing.

Take a moment to ponder, is there an emotional attachment locked in you needing to be released?

What would bring you to a place of healing grace?

What can you let go of that will bring you the experience of God's unconditional love from the inside out?

Perfectly Imperfect Love

As my heart opened to loving myself, layer after layer of forgiveness, jealousy, judgment, self-loathing, and regret all came to the surface to be released. I came to a place of acceptance of every experience I've had throughout my life. Every choice I've made has formed who I am today. I know and embrace who I am. I truly love myself now more than I have ever throughout my previous five decades. This doesn't mean I am completely free of the negative characteristics creeping back in, but now at least I recognize them as tools to help me release another layer.

Throughout my sixtieth-birthday week, I attended a week-long training in Medicinal Aromatherapy in Sedona, Arizona. We students were given the assignment to gaze at ourselves in a mirror and repeat the phrase, "I am a magnificent sovereign being of Divine love." The suggestion was to stop when/if a word became stuck and meditate only on the feelings arising from that particular word. The word I became stuck on was "sovereign." I could not see myself as sovereign. Only God was sovereign. At one point during the week, the "aha" moment came to the surface after hearing someone speak up about her rape.

We were practicing active listening and coaching techniques using essential oils. I was given two blessed souls in my practice group, who helped me process what came to the surface as I relived my rape experience. Even though I had worked through layers of forgiveness of myself and the perpetrator, I couldn't see myself as sovereign. I still saw an imperfect human. I finally released myself from believing I was separate from God and truly embraced God is within me. We are one, co-creating this life which is perfectly imperfect. Using Black Pepper helped bring forth this message:

I am here to show you an all-encompassing love, one that transcends the love you currently understand. This love comes from deep within and is in all existence. I am even encompassing those who do not display love. Send this love to all beings everywhere. As you transcend this three-dimensional existence, know you are working with others to heal the broken-hearted. Assure those who come into your awareness that they are loved and protected by those beings whom they cannot see. Send all comfort and reassurance that the Universe is surrounding them and their families with love. See their faces. Hear their cries. Engulf them with love. Transcend the three-dimensional world whenever a person or group of people grab your attention. This is very important work. It is part of your calling to bring others to this vibrational level. This is a crucial time of healing the separation that exists. The angels are here to assist on many levels. Trust and believe.

I encourage you to engage in this soulful work. Are you able to see yourself as perfectly imperfect, or are you stuck in a pattern of condemning yourself needlessly? I encourage you to try the exercise described above. Standing in front of a mirror, look yourself in the eyes and say "I am a magnificent sovereign being of Divine love." Notice any words you may stumble on and ponder why. With all of my heart, I believe I am a magnificent sovereign being of Divine love and SO ARE YOU!

Living by Grace, Not Perfection

Fear is a stumbling block for many, including me. Much of my fear comes from the early teachings that took hold as described earlier in this chapter. A Course In Miracles, a publication of The Foundation for Inner Peace, teaches that fear is the opposite of love. Where did fear come from, anyway? Perhaps fear is one more of those learning opportunities humans can choose to use as their motivator or oppressor. When fear arises for me now, I step back and look closely at where it is coming from. I personally don't believe in a place called "Hell" but I do believe we can live in "Hell" by the choices we make around fear. If fear is present, rather than becoming debilitated by it, I choose to recognize its existence and then I sit in silence until I can make peace with it. Sometimes, I need to coexist with fear for a while, before revelations appear. Laurel Leaf is my go-to essential oil for bringing me the courage to face my fears. This is one message from Laurel Leaf:

Check in with any discomfort you experience as it comes from the fear of betrayal (more than likely, this stems from past-life experiences). Your intentions have always come from a place of deep love for others and the desire to help them on their healing journey--mind body and spirit. There is no place for fear when you live from the place of Divine love. The Universe is with you. You have a team of unseen supporters who are here to protect you. You need all experiences to help you understand the depth of feelings that exist in humankind. Trust and believe in your inner guidance and move forward with Divine love.

At times, moving forward with Divine love can be easier said than done. As I feel my Inner Guide, God, call me to do something like write this book, create a class, or offer a retreat, and I feel fear creeping in, I simply ask fear: *"What are you here to teach me today?"* Oftentimes I hear the voice of my inner Critic, Ego (remember? Edging God Out), spewing off a list of reasons why I shouldn't take the next step. When this pattern emerges, I courageously take the first step. You see, it doesn't matter if I fail or if I don't think I have what it takes. The inspiration was put there for a reason, and I am to act on it. As long as I am operating from a place of Divine love, anything is possible.

What courageous step do you need to take to add more love in your life?

Is your Ego holding you back?

Are you able to step out anyway and live by grace, not perfection? If not, why not?

If so, how can bringing more grace into your daily life benefit you?

Nature Teaches Unconditional Love

"Study nature, love nature, stay close to nature.
It will never fail you." Frank Lloyd Wright (Wright, 2020)

I have made many "mistakes" in my life, and I imagine I will make many more. As I have grown to trust that I am a Divine extension of God, I believe whatever regrettable actions I've taken or regretful words I've spoken are all part of a Divine plan beyond my wildest imagination. It doesn't absolve me from humbly admitting my mistakes and making amends whenever possible. It simply gives me a different perspective on each situation. I believe we are all spiritual beings on a human path, and we are here to learn and grow from this human experience. If we were perfect, we wouldn't need to be here. This opens us up to acceptance, and acceptance opens us up to feel the unconditional Love of the Universe. On one of my nature treks, Myrtle brought forth a beautiful message:

I am taking you deep within nature. As you are present in nature, take in the feelings as you are looking around. Be the person you see, not an observer of the person you see. What do you feel as you stand here taking in the essence, the energy of nature that is surrounding you? That enfolding of love, feeling wrapped and supported by pure love, is what nature feels at all times throughout life, even in times of transition. We don't feel sad or afraid or resist. We know in our passing we will offer something different and we will contribute love to other beings. This feeling of being surrounded with love is what God desires for all beings, especially human beings, to experience. When it occurs, there will be no separation or division. Be the messenger!

I was immediately reminded of Lynn; Lynn was a messenger to me. She was one of the Teaching Assistants of my Level Two Medicinal Aromatherapy training in Sedona. At the time of the training, this book had lain dormant for eight years. I had been journaling, but I didn't see the correlation between my journaling and my book. It was through her beautiful words that my heart and eyes opened to see clearly my next step. She said, "Take time to be in nature EVERY day! Even if it is only for ten minutes. Nature has so much to tell us. Take time to listen. BE in nature!" Even though she was speaking to our whole class, I felt as though she was looking at me the whole time, directing her message to me. Her message was instrumental and helped open my heart to the teachings of Nature. God's creation has taught me to know that love is what animates life as it moves gracefully and purposefully fulfilling its role. Herein lies the enfolding of love from our Creator.

Do you take time to enjoy nature every day? This can be as simple as walking alone, listening to and observing nature around you. Or as simple as leaning up against a tree (by the way, they love that!). Perhaps your bond will come from a bouquet of flowers or a plant in your home or office. The most important thing is to take at least ten minutes each day to immerse yourself in the natural world and contemplate in silence, free of any distractions. You, too, will become a messenger of love, perhaps for yourself, or perhaps for the entire world. See the love you are through the eyes of nature!

Meditation

Healing Grace

Begin to center yourself for this practice by taking a few deep breaths. Release any tension that may be residing within your body, release any thoughts and concerns of your day, become totally present in this moment. Become one with your life as you relax into our practice.

Imagine your favorite place in nature. If you can't think of one, use your imagination to make one up. Look around you. Visualize the textures and colors surrounding you. Breathe in the fresh, crisp air. Become absorbed in the natural sounds creating a symphony around you. Feel completely peaceful and full of anticipation for the time you are gifting yourself. As you are contemplating life, listen to the questions arising deep within you. Perhaps you are feeling awkward, not knowing what to expect. Perhaps you are hurting and are looking for some relief or comfort. Perhaps you are feeling guilt or shame over a situation. Perhaps the fiery energy of anger and frustration is burning bright and distracting you. Whatever emerges, allow it to be present. Acknowledging it helps to soften the edges just a little bit.

Absorb the energy of the natural surroundings you've created in your mind's eye, witness firsthand how nature appears to be in complete harmony. Notice the natural flow occurring all around you bringing you a sense of awe and wonder. Can you, too, be a part of a natural flow? Can you, too, live in harmony with all that surrounds you in your life?

Take in each of the elements of nature … air, water, earth, fire, and space … realize you are composed of all of the same elements. Is it possible that the Divine Source which is animating all of the natural world is also within you?

This profound insight fills you with joy. You are bathed in a deep, loving energy as you recognize that you are one small thread in this tapestry of life ... along with the vibrancy of nature surrounding you. You sense the uncomfortable emotions are washing away and you are bathed in a compassionate love surpassing anything you've experienced thus far.

As you begin to bring your awareness back to the space you are occupying, your heart swells with the sense of joy and love. Realize you've received one of the biggest gifts of the universe, grace ... healing grace, and all is well with your soul.

When you are ready, slowly open your eyes and carry grace with you into your life. If emotional turmoil disrupts this feeling of grace, simply return to your sanctuary in nature.

Essential Oil Message
Review from Chapter 10

Joy, Love and Amazing Grace

Tamarack

I bring you joy. Remember to feel joy throughout all situations... the kind of joy you feel when you are with your grandchildren or someone special to you. Joy with family. Joy with places that challenge you. Joy with winter. Joy in the beauty of nature. Always be aware of JOY!

Listen with your heart. Embrace all of life's experiences with joy, not judgment. Connect with nature on a deeper level. All of nature is here to guide you, bringing beauty to the earth. Enjoy its beauty. It is true many plants and trees don't belong in certain areas. Nature brings beauty wherever it lives, even if only for a short season. Be mindful and be grateful. Then all of God's creation is happy.

Violet

I am a gentle love opener. I bring new life to you as love grows and emanates from you. I am here to calm fears, mend the broken-hearted, and heal blocks to giving and receiving love.

Black Pepper

I am here to show you an all-encompassing love, one that transcends the love you currently understand. This love comes from deep within and is in all existence. I am even encompassing those who do not display love. Send this love to all beings everywhere. As you transcend this three-dimensional existence, know you are working with others to heal the broken-hearted. Assure those who come into your awareness that they are loved and protected by those beings whom they cannot see. Send all comfort and reassurance that the Universe is surrounding them and their families with love. See their faces. Hear their cries. Engulf them with love. Transcend the three-dimensional world whenever a person or group of people grab your attention. This is very important work. It is part of your calling to bring others to this vibrational level. This is a crucial time of healing the separation that exists. The angels are here to assist on many levels. Trust and believe.

Laurel Leaf

Check in with any discomfort you experience as it comes from the fear of betrayal (more than likely, this stems from past-life experiences). Your intentions have always come from a place of deep love for others and the desire to help them on their healing journey--mind body and spirit. There is no place for fear when you live from the place of Divine love. The Universe is with you. You have a team of unseen supporters who are here to protect you. You need all experiences to help you understand the depth of feelings that exist in humankind. Trust and believe in your inner guidance and move forward with Divine love.

Myrtle

I am taking you deep within nature. As you are present in nature, take in the feelings as you are looking around. Be the person you see, not an observer of the person you see. What do you feel as you stand here taking in the essence, the energy of nature that is surrounding you? That enfolding of love, feeling wrapped and supported by pure love, is what nature feels at all times throughout life, even in times of transition. We don't feel sad or afraid or resist. We know in our passing we will offer something different and we will contribute love to other beings. This feeling of being surrounded with love is what God desires for all beings, especially human beings, to experience. When it occurs, there will be no separation or division. Be the messenger!

"Take time to be in nature EVERY DAY! Even if it is only for 10 minutes. Nature has so much to tell us. Take time to listen. Be in nature!" Lynn (Wisdom of the Earth Level 2 Teaching Assistant)

White Fences

White fences

Are we inside or out?

It is safe and secure on the inside

But there is so much to discover out there

I will choose to go out

And see the world

From outside

White fences.

-2007

Chapter 11

Trust

"In the woods we return to reason and faith."
Ralph Waldo Emerson (Emerson, 2020)

If You Want to Make God Laugh, Tell Him Your Plans

The above message, print on a small card, was given to me by a friend who saw my struggle as a recovering control freak. It was posted on the wall of my office as my daily reminder. At the time, I paid so much attention to detail in planning that when life threw me a curve ball, I nearly lost my mind. I thought I was making life easier by my attentiveness to detail. One summer, I planned a 21-day trip out West covering 6,000 miles with my first husband and our two boys. Needless-to-say, when we arrived at Mount Rushmore on a foggy day and were scheduled to be in Yellowstone the next evening, I wasn't a happy camper. Each experience brought me closer to trusting in the beauty of spontaneity.

My second husband introduced me to spontaneity. Early in our relationship, he told me he was taking his two kids to Puerto Rico, and he invited me to join them. Endless beaches, hiking through a rainforest, steamy tropical climate--sounds great, right? The catch: he planned on going in two days! I had the responsibilities of my full-time job, I had to keep the fundraising committee on-task for an upcoming auction I was overseeing, and I had my part-time job all on the schedule. My peers encouraged, actually pushed, me to drop everything and GO! That experience was the opening to a new way of maneuvering through life and has continued into the life we have created together.

It was in the spring of 2006, a few years into that new marriage, when I experienced the most profound opportunity to fall into the arms of trust. We had decided to put both of our houses on the market and build a new home where we could start our life together in fresh surroundings. We purchased a lot and began the construction process, serving as our own general contractors. We used the house I owned as a rental property. My tenants had carelessly caused a fire, leading us into a restoration process at the same time we were building. I was feeling quite humbled by my inexperience and lack of landlord skills, and I was embarrassed by the filth the tenants had left behind. Through an ad, we found a young man to clean out the debris and belongings left behind by the tenants, enough to fill a 20-yard dumpster. On the day I met him to go over what needed to be done, I was exhausted and self-conscious of my home in shambles. As he began to drive away, he stopped and recited, "*So we do not lose heart. Even though our outer nature is wasting away, our inner nature is being renewed day by day. For this slight momentary affliction is preparing us for an eternal weight of glory beyond all measure, because we look not at what can be seen but at what cannot be seen; for what can be seen is temporary, but what cannot be seen is eternal. 2 Corinthians 4:16-18 (NRSV).* Trust me, ma'am, everything will be alright." No doubt, he was an angel in human form bringing me the lesson of trust.

By the end of the same summer, one week before school started, we were scheduled to close on my husband's house, the house we were living in. However, my house was in the renovation process and our new house was more than ten days from completion. All attempts to make the transition flow smoothly backfired. I had meticulously scheduled every detail, but the plans began falling apart. I clearly remember the feeling of panic my body, mind, and spirit felt at the time. On the morning of the closing, I hadn't finished packing. I awoke to a message from my sister that my parents' apartment complex had experienced a fire and they were temporarily displaced at her home. In addition, our arrangement to rent a cabin from a friend had fallen through. Yet the closing was scheduled for 10:00 a.m. As we pulled out of the driveway, I remember totally surrendering and saying to God, *I give up.*

The closing itself is a blur in my mind. I know I was there physically, but I was not engaged at any other level. After the closing, when we were in the parking lot, our realtor (a friend of my husband) asked us what our plans were. Upon hearing our dilemma, he told us we were welcome to stay at his house. Another angel appearing in human form teaching me to trust!

Even though these experiences have taught me to fall back into the arms of trust, I have to admit I still get caught up in planning; however, the curve balls aren't quite as daunting as they once were. And I have the beloved essences and meditation to help channel the reminders of the force constantly moving through life. I can trust that

God's got my back. Artemisia Titepati clearly brought forth a message to help me remember to trust:

Good day, Beloved One! I'm here to remind you to relax and let go. You are exactly where you need to be at this moment. We are all preparing the way, and it will be clear when the time is right. All signs that are unfolding are there to make it an easier transition when the Divine time is right. Trust and believe. Rely on the beautiful essences to escort you through the challenging, uncomfortable times. We are all here to support you. This will be effortless on your part. Trust and believe.

Trusting in a Divine plan can be unsettling, even intimidating. Through the many experiences I've encountered in my life, I am learning to make peace with those disturbing feelings. Who am I to think I have the *best* possible plan? I am not suggesting we sit back and do nothing to prepare in life, however, we need to leave space for something better to come to us.

Can you recall a time in your life when you were holding on tightly but chose to surrender and then something better than you expected came your way?

Were you able to step back and fall into the arms of trust?

Opening ourselves up to *receive* whatever the universe has to offer may take us out of our comfort zone. Are you willing to forfeit your independence to a power greater than yourself?

Inner Guidance Positioning System

We were all born with the natural ability to grow, change, and become something different from our original form. Of course! Otherwise, we would all be stuck in the newborn phase. Each stage and experience we go through brings us to a new level of awareness. Our inner GPS is continually being downloaded and updated. Our physical form learned to move first by rolling over, then by inching forward, and eventually by learning to stand. Once we had reached the upright position, curiosity took over and we began to explore our world. Throughout these stages, most of us had adult support and encouragement. Every cell within our bodies absorbed the new information, updated the database, sent out the necessary signals, and readjusted to accommodate our new position. This intricate system operated without much intervention from the outside world. If our physical system works so synchronically, why don't we rely on our inner GPS when it comes to decision making and living a fulfilling life?

Several decades of my life were spent acquiring information in many ways. Continuing education was a requirement for both of my careers, and often my interest in courses or reading was sparked simply for self-improvement. I always thought I needed to learn more. If I wasn't an "expert" on the topic, I relied on other sources to educate me. I continually turned to outside sources to gather information, oftentimes struggling to find balance within my schedule. I became reliant on facts provided by other people. But what if, instead, I had simply turned inward? I wonder how much information is available to us through our inner GPS, just as it was programmed in our early stages of life to move us into our next stages of development? Learning is part of my nature. I love learning. However, there were many times when I allowed my lack of knowledge to become a frustration. Recently I came across this quote from seventeenth-century Dutch philosopher Baruch Spinoza: "The more you struggle to live, the less you live. Give up the notion that you must be sure of what you are doing. Instead, surrender to what is real within you, for that alone is sure…you are above everything distressing." The line "surrender to what is real within you, for that alone is sure" spoke volumes to me, as I had lived much of my life not trusting what I knew to be true within me. I had allowed the information fed to me by others to overrule what I innately believed to be true within. Artemisia Titepati helped affirm this for me:

Books and readings are one tool that will spark remembrances, but you don't have to search for the answers. They are already there. You have all you need within you. You know all that you need to know. Trust and believe, my Beloved.

This is a much easier concept to grasp when I'm not the one trying to live it. Here, again, living in the place of trust rather than control is key. For me, so many of my deep learning opportunities came through my experiences rather than from one manual or another. When I trust my inner GPS to be my guide, life is much less distressing.

Consider the circumstances within your own life. Are you trying too hard to search for the correct answers?

Tune into your inner GPS. What is it telling you?

Hold the Vision, Trust the Process

When I coach clients who are feeling stuck, uncertain of what they want in life or unclear of which direction to go, we begin by looking at what they are passionate about. Sometimes they are in a career that is in alignment with their passions, but many times they are not. I am not suggesting that everyone should quit their job if it is unfulfilling. However, it is crucial for us to hold the vision of what inspires us, trusting in the process it takes to get us there. Too often, our thoughts become our roadblocks. If we keep thinking "I need the benefits," "I depend on my income," "My passions won't provide a substantial income," then we will bring to fruition what we believe to be true. But the opposite is also possible. Creatively visualizing ourselves living our dreams and visions will clear the negativity and open us up to endless possibilities. As we discover our soul purpose, we are emboldened, rooted in our unique place, to offer gifts to the world around us. My passion is to guide people to their soul's purpose so they can live from their unique place and offer their gifts to the world around them.

I, too, have struggled with trusting in the process. The path less followed isn't always an easy path to navigate. Obstacles and diversions are a sure sign that I've strayed from holding the vision. When I was clearly guided to proceed with this book but didn't have a clue as to how it would unfold, I tried to set aside time to meditate and reflect on the deep desire welling up inside of me. However, I allowed myself to take on too many projects for others and found it increasingly difficult to find the time for myself. I became irritated and edgy whenever meetings were called to discuss the projects. Because I was over-committed, I lowered my standards and only half-heartedly fulfilled my obligations. I knew I should walk away from these projects, but I didn't, afraid my reputation might be tainted if I gave up.

The lesson I took away from that particular experience has helped me to trust my instincts. When something feels forced and not aligned with what my spirit is calling me to do, I now politely decline and walk away. No guilt. No pressure to comply. It is truly empowering to reclaim your power and not give it away to others.

As I write this, there are a plethora of uncertainties with how this book will come into its completed form. I can choose to hold onto the vision and trust the process, or I can get caught up in trying to figure it out by myself. So far, everything I've needed has been provided. If you are reading this, the project has come to fruition without my need to force it. A message from my beloved essence, Marjoram, is my go-to when I fall into feeling the need to control:

See your future but do not attach to it. See yourself doing what you love to do. There is no need to figure out the details. Life will come naturally and effortlessly. The more control you try to take, the harder it will be for you. You have a whole team paving the way. Trust, allow, and believe. You will know without a doubt what action you need to take. Enjoy the present moment and be grateful for it!

Are there obstacles seemingly holding back your vision?

Reflect on your efforts. Is it possible that other diversions are preventing your vision from manifesting?

Or perhaps, you may be in a time when you don't have a clear vision. Be okay with waiting as it may be time for a pause. Trust the process to unfold no matter what you are experiencing.

Meditation

Trusting in the Flow of Life

Our Sacral Chakra is located in the region of our body just below the navel and above the pubic bone. This chakra, when fully opened, is our place of creativity and procreation, helping us create the beautiful life we desire. Think of the flow of water with the tides as it ebbs and flows. Think of a gentle flowing river as it meanders here and there.

When this chakra is imbalanced, guilt tends to be present in some form, preventing us from moving forward to create the life we desire. Guilt because we haven't accomplished what we expected. Guilt because we don't believe we deserve what we have. Guilt from old tapes from our past. Guilt that we aren't doing enough.

To be at a place where we can create and flow with life, we must let go of guilt. We embrace courage, we trust we are exactly where we need to be, we find a place of gratitude for all of our life's experiences thus far. We begin to feel free and unrestricted. All reservations fade.

As you begin to prepare for this meditation, take a moment to relax and breathe into the space just below your navel. Feel the gentle rise and fall with each breath. Surrender to your breath … allow thoughts to drift through. Send the breath to areas that may feel tight, and allow yourself to relax and release just a little bit more.

Imagine yourself lying on a beach near the ocean. Notice your breath becoming one with the flow of the waves. Feel the gentle movement within your body, just as the water flows. You envision a beautiful orange glow … like a sunset … surrounding you.

As your body surrenders to the flow, you notice the orange energy gently encompassing you ... bringing a spark to your creativity that has been dormant, waiting for this moment.

This spark ignites within you a sense of courage ... you see exactly what you want to create in your life. As your courage builds and the vision of where you will be next strengthens ... you have a sense of overwhelming trust ... knowing the universe will take you there ... providing you with exactly what you need when you need it. Your whole being pulses with a deep sense of gratitude ... and you are at peace.

Gently bring your awareness back to your Sacral Chakra area and focus on your breath, allowing it to flow naturally as you observe it ... know you are fully supported and energized to move forward with trust ... know life is bringing you exactly what you need, when you need it.

When you are ready, open your eyes and embrace your journey forward.

Essential Oil Message
Review from Chapter 11

Trust

Artemisia Titepati

Good day, Beloved One! I'm here to remind you to relax and let go. You are exactly where you need to be at this moment. We are all preparing the way, and it will be clear when the time is right. All signs that are unfolding are there to make it an easier transition when the Divine time is right. Trust and believe. Rely on the beautiful essences to escort you through the challenging, uncomfortable times. We are all here to support you. This will be effortless on your part. Trust and believe.

Books and readings are one tool that will spark remembrances, but you don't have to search for the answers. They are already there. You have all you need within you. You know all that you need to know. Trust and believe, my Beloved.

Marjoram

See your future, but do not attach to it. See yourself doing what you love to do. There is no need to figure out the details. Life will unfold naturally and effortlessly. The more control you try to take, the harder it will be for you. You have a whole team paving the way. Trust, allow, and believe. You will know without a doubt what action you need to take. Enjoy the present moment and be grateful for it!

Chapter 12

Soul Resilience

"Every flower is a soul blossoming in nature."
Gerard de Nerval (Nerval, 2020)

Belonging

There is a saying, "people are in your life for a reason, a season, or a lifetime". Throughout this past decade, it has been important to me to align with my heart and not forego what I believe just to keep people in my life. I left a place where I had allowed my entire identity to be consumed. I found I had been trying to rescue the people who were close to me. However, they couldn't see what I saw. They were content in their ways and didn't seem to want to grow or change. I led programs, I introduced new concepts, I gave personal testimonials of life-changing experiences, each time, thinking *this* would surely inspire someone. The more experience I had with developing my spirituality, the more I wanted to share it with my peers. God was calling me to speak out and step out boldly in an environment where I felt I no longer belonged. The inner conflict I experienced brought me healing: healing from the feeling of being alone in the world, from my own judgments, from my own failings at being impeccable with my word. It also provided me with the opportunity to truly embrace and live the Truth as I believed it in my heart.

One morning as I was meditating with Artemisia Titepati, a beautiful butterfly circled around me and landed on the inspirational book I had been reading. She also landed on me several times while I journaled the message that was streaming through me to my pen:

You are part of a larger "tribe." You have felt you don't belong where you are, but for now this is where you need to be. You need to train others to be healers. Your "tribe" is always with you, in many forms. A visitor from nature is your physical confirmation of this. Pay attention. Your time is limited where you are. Be diligent, mindful, and present while you are there. Your impact will make a difference in that community.

This Silver-Spotted Skipper butterfly came back several times that morning. She even landed on my nose! Her visit was such a joyful reminder of how our true tribe is much greater than our perceived circle.

Who makes up your tribe?

Have you experienced a time in your life when you felt you were outgrowing the circle of people you were connected to?

In what ways were you able to stand in your Truth and leave behind anything that no longer resonated?

Do you WANT to nurture the feeling of loneliness?

Have you been drawn to a new tribe? If so, why do you think this is happening?

Readjusting Through Energy Shifts

I find travel can throw my energy off. This also happens to my husband. It seems each of us goes through an energy shift when we have been apart for a few days or more so that when we reunite adjustment is necessary. This unhealthy pattern happens in our relationship: When my husband challenges me in any way, I hold my ground. We disagree and I remove myself or shut down. And the reverse is true... if I challenge him, he holds his ground and we disagree. As we engage in this habitual pattern, I tend to become less careful with my words. As I meditated with Peppermint, light was shed on this subject:

> *Withdraw from your senses and you will be able to connect with the universe with ease. Allow my scent to take you to a deeper place within. As you inhale, follow how deep I go within you. Feel me in your heart. In the past, you've only brushed the surface of the depth of love that is there for you. Your Creator wants you to experience this with the snap of a finger so when you are being faced with challenging situations, you can go deeply in an instant. You will be guided. Old patterns surface easily, but help is always available to support you through a new way of being.*

Ponder the ways in which you are equipped to go out into the world and make a difference through your life's experiences. What are your special gifts?

What patterns might be present that are blocking your special gifts?

Are you ready to release them?

In what way can nature assist you as you strive to release old patterns?

Turbulence or Stillness?

Throughout this past decade, my husband and I have experienced many shifts and changes in our personal and our professional lives. We became empty nesters as our two youngest children finished college and began life on their own. My oldest son got married and started a family, blessing me with two beautiful grandchildren. Our careers have slowly dissolved as my husband was laid off at 63 years old. At this stage in life, he can't see himself pushing to land a new company to work for and starting all over from scratch. And for me, Novel Coronavirus has brought my massage career to a screeching halt.

It has always been my husband's dream to live in a warm climate when he retires. He doesn't do well in our climate as he likes to be active outside cycling, hiking, canoeing, and such. Our garden becomes our haven throughout the summer months, and we enthusiastically reap the benefits of our labors in the fall. In our cold winter months, we have found respite in the Caribbean for a week each November and March, fishing, snorkeling, and kayaking.

However, I now have grandchildren who are an important part of my life, and I don't want to be their "absent" grandma. Moving South would require us to leave half of our family behind. It is a dilemma neither one of us perceived would become an obstacle. On a good day, I can relax into the flow of life trusting in the Divine energy that animates all. On a not-so-good day, I feel apprehensive about where our future will take us. Given we are both Aries, our headstrongness and desire to be the lead makes it challenging for us to compromise.

It was on one of those not-so-good days that Ocean Pine brought forth a brilliant message which I go back to often:

As you take in the love and energy of Ocean Pine, notice the sensations within your body. That place of complete wholeness and stillness is because you are in a space that is best aligned for you. This is what your Creator desires for you, to feel complete and still, as this is when your spirit will be able to manifest more. Blessings abound wherever you are. There is no need to worry about the details. All of this will happen gently and with total love surrounding you. Enjoy today!

Indeed, it is in the stillness when I feel my soul connection come alive and I'm at peace and one with life. Blessings truly do abound wherever we are and worry keeps us in a lower vibrational flow. I needed the reminder that I am complete and whole wherever I am.

Are you able to find stillness wherever you are?

Where do you feel most aligned?

Are you able to tap into the space of feeling complete and still?

If not, what would it take to get you there?

Your Life Is Sacred

Whether or not you follow a religious or spiritual path, your life is sacred. I believe a loving God created us as individuals and has given us the freedom to choose what we will do with this one precious life we've been given. I wholeheartedly believe the saying "We are spiritual beings on an earthly path, not earthly beings on a spiritual path." Somehow, in some way, we were given the miraculous opportunity to be brought into this world we know. If you have any doubts about this at all, I would suggest you search "fertilization" on

YouTube. Watching the process unfold is fascinating, and you will see how life is truly miraculous.

I took this concept of fertilization for granted, as many of us do, until I saw a simulation video on the process of conception and fertilization. I had already conceived and given birth to my two sons, which I did believe was miraculous, but seeing the simulation of the fertilization process brought me a whole new appreciation for the miracle of life. I was enthralled by the fact that there are millions of sperm released each time in the process of intercourse, and as they "swim" towards the egg, it is up to the cells surrounding the egg to determine whether or not one of millions will be allowed to break through, thus beginning the cycle of new life. But this process isn't exclusive to humans. It happens in the plant world through pollination and in the tree world through spores and seeds. Procreation is a sacred part of life, and it is all around us.

Peia Luzzi is a musician and recording artist who specializes in sacred chants that are inspiring. One song by Peia entitled "Blessed We Are" speaks to the sacredness of life. I recommend listening closely to the lyrics. The sacred essence of Spikenard brought forth a message speaking to this sacredness of life:

> *Remember why you came here. Your life is sacred. All of life is sacred. Remember that in everything you do. Remember that with every person you meet. You are holy and loved beyond what your human capacity can understand. There is a sacred force moving you through life. Yes, you will encounter forces that will try to throw you off track. Recognize this. Honor them for the role or lessons they bring, and send them off with unconditional love. You may not always have someone to help you through difficult situations. Turn to nature in your times*

of unsettledness and ask what you need to know. God is work-
ing with you on deeper levels, and these opportunities to grow
will come more rapidly. As you learn to rely on the universe,
your path forward will be revealed. Bless you and the lives you
will touch.

I encourage you to take time to ponder the sacredness of life. Tap into the unconditional love available to all. Use your times of unsettledness to go deeper into your sacred life and see what emerges for you.

In what ways do you honor your sacredness?

Are you able to see ALL individuals and all beings as sacred?

Dis-ease of the Spiritual Heart

No doubt, we have all encountered a situation in which we were among a group of strangers and quickly became aware of their political and/or religious differences. It can be quite awkward and unsettling as you navigate from one person to the next only to discover there really isn't a conversation you want to engage in. For me, this becomes a trigger for my judgment to kick into high gear, even though I practice letting go of differences, and the acceptance of all individuals' choices.

This happened to me last summer as I was celebrating someone's anniversary and significant birthday. I wanted to leave. I wanted to run away. I began looking at each person and, in my self-righteousness, the judging began: "How could *they* profess to be Christians? Why don't *they* see our current president for the lying crook he is? Look at them, no wonder *they* are able to engage in conversations with one another." Of course, the following morning, as I reflected on all that had transpired and my feelings associated with it, Goldenrod brought forth a much-needed message:

I am here to reveal dis-ease of your spiritual heart. Our message from the plant and tree kingdom is to be like us, filled with unconditional love and releasing all judgment. We do not judge humans for the devastation and destruction that has been done to us. We know that it is part of a greater plan. Your role is not to convince others that you are right and they are wrong. Your role is to stand in your integrity of what you believe to be true. To release judgment means to accept and respect others exactly where they are in this lifetime. It does not mean you need to remain silent, but it also does not mean you have to prove your place of authenticity is accurate and theirs isn't. Use these uncomfortable situations as practice to become more self-assured and confident in your response. These are all learning and growing opportunities. Bless you for your openness to learn and grow.

Thank God for grace, as I go through this uncomfortable process of growing and learning. In the moment, it is not easy for me to feel self-assured and confident. Letting go of my need to be right is key to finding the place of balance in those uncomfortable situations. As I begin to tune into my body's response more, I am becoming aware of the deep-seated changes I need to implement. It is okay for others to think differently than I do. They, too, are sacred beings on this planet working through whatever they came here to work through. Some may be aware and some may not. Ultimately it doesn't matter. What matters most is for me to work through the changes *I* need to make within myself to unconditionally love others and release judgment.

Uncomfortable situations arise for all of us. If you were to rate yourself on the "I judge this much" scale, where would you be?

Are you aware of how much judging you do of others, or does judgment surface so automatically you aren't even aware?

I encourage you to spend time pondering those uncomfortable situations you have experienced. Then, ask yourself: Am I truly loving this person or situation unconditionally?

If the answer is "yes," great! If the answer is "no," take time to ponder ways in which you can shift your mindset to one of expansive love, unconditional love, seeing ALL beings as sacred.

Meditation

Interconnectedness of Life

Find a comfortable position, allowing your body to be fully supported. Relax into the rhythm of your breath. As you breathe in, feel the energy filling you. As you exhale, feel every muscle, every fiber, relaxing.

Breathing in energy, contentment, positivity. Exhaling and releasing frustrations, obstacles, fears.

Imagine the energy of the sunshine, warm on your face and your skin. As you breathe in, you find yourself near the ocean. Listen to the songs of the birds and the sound of the waves gently lapping along the shore. You are basking in the warmth, smiling, and enjoying the peace of the moment. Inhaling, smell the saltiness of the ocean as it brings you a feeling of belonging.

Gaze out at the waves and imagine you are one of them, gently floating along sparkling as the sunshine glows on you. You look around and you see all of the other waves gently moving and sparkling and you are filled with wonder and awe as you realize you are all connected. One flowing into another. One reaching out to the other.

As far as you can see, there is a sea of waves. Quiet. Calm. Gentle. Sparkling.

Bring your attention back to where you are, sitting on the warm sand. Curl your toes and feel your feet sinking into the warmth. You are filled with wonder and awe at the millions of particles burying your feet. Smile as you feel so connected with creation and you realize you, too, have a purpose for existing, for being alive.

You are as gentle as the waves.

You have a sparkling personality.

You are warm and all-embracing.

You are one small part working and living together with others.

And all is good.

Gently bring your awareness back to the space you are occupying. Feel your body as you begin to move mindfully. Bring your awareness to your breath. Notice the energy now coursing through every fiber of your being, filling you with contentment and joy. Embrace this experience for as long as you need.

When you are ready, slowly open your eyes and see the world through the interconnectedness with all life you encountered, your deep soul connection.

Essential Oil Message
Review from Chapter 12

Soul Connection

Artemisia, Titepati

You are part of a larger "tribe." You have felt you don't belong where you are, but for now this is where you need to be. You need to train others to be healers. Your "tribe" is always with you, in many forms. A visitor from nature is your physical confirmation of this. Pay attention. Your time is limited where you are. Be diligent, mindful, and present while you are there. Your impact will make a difference in that community.

Peppermint

Withdraw from your senses and you will be able to connect with the universe with ease. Allow my scent to take you to a deeper place within. As you inhale, follow how deep I go within you. Feel me in your heart. In the past, you've only brushed the surface of the depth of love that is there for you. Your Creator wants you to experience this with the snap of a finger so when you are being faced with challenging situations, you can go deeply in an instant. You will be guided. Old patterns surface easily, but help is always available to support you through a new way of being.

Ocean Pine

As you take in the love and energy of Ocean Pine, notice the sensations within your body. That place of complete wholeness and stillness is because you are in a space that is best aligned for you. This is what your Creator desires for you, to feel complete and still, as this is when your spirit will be able to manifest more. Blessings abound wherever you are. There is no need to worry about the details. All of this will happen gently and with total love surrounding you. Enjoy today!

Spikenard

Remember why you came here. Your life is sacred. All of life is sacred. Remember that in everything you do. Remember that with every person you meet. You are holy and loved beyond what your human capacity can understand. There is a sacred force moving you through life. Yes, you will encounter forces that will try to throw you off track. Recognize this. Honor them for the role or lessons they bring, and send them off with unconditional love. You may not always have someone to help you through difficult situations. Turn to nature in your times of unsettledness and ask what you need to know. God is working with you on deeper levels, and these opportunities to grow will come more rapidly. As you learn to rely on the universe, your path forward will be revealed. Bless you and the lives you will touch.

Goldenrod

I am here to reveal dis-ease of your spiritual heart. Our message from the plant and tree kingdom is to be like us, filled with unconditional love and releasing all judgment. We do not judge humans for the devastation and destruction that has been done to us. We know that it is part of a greater plan. Your role is not to convince others that you are right and they are wrong. Your role is to stand in your integrity of what you believe to be true. To release judgment means to accept and respect others exactly where they are in this lifetime. It does not mean you need to remain silent, but it also does not mean you have to prove your place of authenticity is accurate and theirs isn't. Use these uncomfortable situations as practice to become more self-assured and confident in your response. These are all learning and growing opportunities. Bless you for your openness to learn and grow.

Chapter 13

Truth

"You are enough, simply in your being."
Jeff Foster (Foster, 2020)

Enough!

One challenge I faced throughout my life was the feeling that I wasn't enough. As a child, I didn't think I was smart enough. As a teen, I wasn't pretty enough. As an adult, I wasn't educated enough. All of this stinking thinking held me back from living my true potential. Or perhaps I needed to experience the not-enough mentality in order to be where I am today? Either way, I've put a lot of energy into healing each of those stages of my life.

When I was school-age, I distinctly remember coming home with my report card, which was neatly sealed in an envelope that only my parents were allowed to open. My mother was the one who opened it, but she never gave it too much attention. She told me to bring it to my dad. The dread began to build as I knew his typical response. True to form, he said, "Is this your best?" and my response was, "I think so." Then he replied, "Well I don't think so. I think you could have done better." So being a "B" average student wasn't good enough in his mind. Try as I did, I just couldn't get to the point of having straight "A's"; therefore, my conclusion was I wasn't smart enough.

Others influenced my thinking as well. There was Mrs. Short, my art teacher kindergarten through second grade. Surely, I could get an "A" in art class, or so I thought. I loved to color and draw pictures. I vividly remember Mrs. Short walking slowly around our table, peering over our shoulders at our work. I was very aware of her nonverbal responses and how her eyes lit up when she saw a drawing she liked. As she moved behind me, I felt like a tight rope ready to coil, wondering what she was thinking. I got a "humph" sound instead of the "ooo" sound she made when she saw something she liked. That response stuck with me until I went back to school when I was in my thirties. I enrolled in a required art class at Alverno College. The first question our professor asked was, "How many of you think you are an artist?" Of course, my hand didn't go up. Then he asked, "How many of you are convinced you are NOT an artist?" Most of the class held their hands up. His next statement eventually changed my life: "Everyone is an artist. Some people are able to make a living by being an artist and others are not. But it doesn't change the fact that EVERYONE is born an artist." Now that is a truth I can believe! I've come to discover how our thoughts distort reality.

Our thoughts can debilitate us or empower us. It's our choice. I found out how much comparisons can get us into trouble. It happens so naturally that we aren't even aware of its effect until years, sometimes decades, later. The truths we take on are what the ego wants us to believe. Many of the self-help books will refer to the truth of the ego as the small "t" truth and the true essence of who we are as the big "T" Truth. Who are we listening to today? Are we listening to the voice of the I'm-not-enough small "t" truth, or are we listening to the voice of the I AM enough big "T" Truth, our True essence?

I do have the tendency to slip into the old patterns of thinking. Clary Sage brought me an affirming message one morning as I had slipped into the lower vibrational energy of the not-enough mentality. I had fallen into the ego trap of thinking I didn't know enough, that I wasn't smart enough to make a viable contribution to our family income. This is what I heard:

> *You can enjoy the peaceful moments of nature at all times. You are trusting the guidance of the plants and trees more and more with each person you encounter. Be in that place at all times. Release the "not enough" mentality that creeps in to distract you. Think abundantly and trust the universe to do the rest. Listen to the still small voice within and follow guidance. You are always supported.*

At times like this I am especially grateful to have a meditation practice. It is in these quiet moments of contemplation when I can return to the still small voice within, connecting me to the Truth of who I really am. I encourage you to seek out your Truth. Take time to discern if the not-enough voice of ego is clouding your ability to hear the voice of your inner Spirit, which is truly who you are.

The Truth of Abundance

I have begun each of the past five years by attending a New Year's Intention-Setting workshop. Several years ago, our facilitator had us do a visualization exercise. She had us write down our perfect day, whatever that meant to each of us. At the time of doing the exercise, my work week was quite full, I devoted one day each week to my grandson, and somehow, I fit in time to teach yoga and extra workshops. Our facilitator encouraged us to let go of the reality of our actual day and instead envision our ideal day. As I pondered my ideal day, I remembered a friend of mine, Judith, who lives in The Bahamas.

Judith is a Canadian, a single woman, an artist, and an entrepreneur. Through a series of life's circumstances, she landed in The Bahamas in a beautiful studio home. Judith lives a woman's dream. She has beautiful tropical gardens, lives a short distance from the crystal clear, turquoise ocean, and is the most welcoming, friendly host to strangers. I've known Judith for eight years, and I've always been intrigued by the life she has created for herself. I know that she faces many challenges and obstacles, works extremely hard, and holds onto an unshakable faith through it all. She has perfected her ideal day with an amazing balance between self-care, creative time, work, and play.

It was with that image in mind that I pondered my perfect day. It included all of the things I loved the most: time for reflection/meditation; time for writing, creating and reading; time in nature and for self-care; time for work, gardening and providing nourishing meals for my family. It was a beautiful vision, and I felt content imagining it. As I returned to my daily life, I tried to make time for my ideal day. With so many obligations, trying to live my vision just added more stress to my already overloaded schedule. Reality took over. I accepted with gratitude the days I could fit in some of the things on my list, and let go of the dream.

The sweet-smelling essence of Davana stepped in to encourage me:

Stand in your power! Be clear and confident in your intention and it will manifest. There will be changes and it may be challenging, but all will go smoothly. Some of those you know will continue on their path with you and others may not. Know that you have given them exactly what they've needed at the time, and they will be led to their next step. You will find abundance coming to you easily and effortlessly in many ways--time for whatever your heart desires. You will receive abundance for your work. Your next best step is being revealed. Use the essences to support your efforts!

I was so focused on making a fair and equitable contribution to our family finances that I had lost sight of the Truth of abundance. All along, I was focused on my small "t" truth--trying to earn enough to meet my obligations, looking at my time as being limited and looking at my resources as being something I controlled. COVID-19 has gifted me with my perfect day. I am now able to walk through my day and I find that abundance is all around me. Occasionally, I get caught in the trap of worrying about the adjustments I've had to make monetarily, but then I realize how much abundance has come my way through these past five months. The Truth of abundance is that there is enough for ALL. I am privileged in this world of ours. I never want to lose sight of that fact. In my abundant life, I can certainly reach out to those who do not have a morsel of sustenance due to the pandemic, droughts, and disasters. It's all about reframing how I think of things. I have had an abundance of opportunities come my way that I would have missed if we weren't in the middle of this pandemic. My heart is filled with gratitude for it all.

What do you see as Truth about abundance?

Can you see the importance of setting your intention to manifest what your True Self, your inner essence, wants to create for you in your perfect day?

Or, perhaps you are already living your perfect day?

From Frigid to Amicable

In 2011, I experienced one of the happiest days of my life: my oldest son's wedding. I felt blessed to see my son so happy and all grown up. His whole life flashed before my eyes as I realized the circle of life goes on. It was a blissful day for me from start to finish. Nothing was going to break through the deep pride I held for him. However, the months leading up to that glorious day were filled with opportunities for me to come to terms with the Truth of who I really was.

It began with his request for me to host a shower for my side of the family, which consisted of three aunts, four nieces, and a couple of family friends. He also said he was asking his step-mom to host one for his dad's side of the family, which had even fewer women. Even though this was over ten years after the divorce from his dad, my son still felt the need to keep us separated. Admittedly, I was quite frigid when it came to my ex, and I'm guessing my son picked up on my energy. However, my desire to heal the negative emotions of judgment and resentment far outweighed holding on to past hurts. It was time to let go and embrace the Truth that ALL beings are Divine love, including those who have challenged us.

As I studied and worked with A Course In Miracles, a line in Lesson #49 has helped me reframe my thinking. I have come to realize that I actually have held a place of love in my heart, even when I wasn't able to feel the love and even when I needed to leave the unhealthy relationship. Sometimes, love has us do the difficult task of moving on. Sometimes, we need to move on in order for the healing to begin. God IS always leading us.

"The part of your mind in which Truth abides is in constant communication with God, whether you are aware of it or not." (Foundation for Inner Peace, 2007)

I reached out to see if my ex's wife would want to collaborate and plan the family bridal shower for my soon-to-be daughter-in-law. To my relief, she said yes! The simple act of reaching out opened the door for me to move through past hurts, find forgiveness which had been buried, and discover the unconditional love, Divine love, that was always there. I was now able to relax into amicability as the wedding preparations unfolded. This was my son's special day, and I didn't want anything to cloud it or burden him, especially my wounds. I was able to converse with my ex and share in the pride that we both felt for our son. I found the place of unconditional love that was there all along, just buried beneath the pile of unhealthy emotions.

When we embark on the difficult task of healing the past hurts and doing the fearless self-inventory, the world around us becomes a better place. The energy lifts, and a feeling of lightness replaces the heaviness. I was able to experience every moment of their wedding day with joy and love and enthusiasm. I floated through the day on the proverbial Cloud Nine. It was a blessed day, indeed!

As I reflected on my life and the twists and turns it has taken, the lively citrus essence of Grapefruit called to me and brought forth this reminder:

The glass is half full. Remember this in all aspects of life, and find gratitude in all things. You have spent time wondering if some information is true and if the deliverers of this information are truly authentic. What does your heart say, not your head? If you believe in God, then believe with all of your heart. If you believe in Guides, then believe with all of your heart. If you believe in Angels and Plants and Trees, then believe with all of your heart. Doubting is a lower energy and not part of the upward spiral you desire in your life. It is possible to believe in all things with all of your heart. To thine own self be true! Remember to always follow and listen to your heart.

We are not always tuned in to recognize that we are following our heart. Sometimes, we take steps because there is an invisible force moving us in a particular direction, as I did in the above story. When we take the time to feel gratitude for not just the common things in life, but also for the opportunities that have brought us immense growth, we open the door to our heart a little bit more. When our heart is opened, we begin to see Truth in a different way, and we can embrace life with love, joy and enthusiasm.

Is there a situation or time in your life that needs to be met with courage and forgiveness?

Who or what is guiding you?

Are you resisting? Why?

Spend some time in quiet reflection. Allow the essence of Grapefruit to help you see the glass as half full, rather than half empty.

Healing from the Inside Out

Nature teaches us resilience. She demonstrates this all around us, if we tune in to her. As with my story of the beloved maple tree who fully recovered from the lightning strike, with a little human assistance (see p.17). Her wounds went deep into her core. Slowly, over time, she mended her internal wounds and radiated life on her surface. If our Creator designed nature with so much resilience, surely, we too are created with the ability to heal from our core, slowly over time. Then we, also, can radiate life around us.

Throughout these pages, I have shared my personal journey of healing from the inside out. No, I wasn't struck by lightning, and I didn't begin with a broken body. The healing I have shared has come from my core, those deeper layers of wounds of the emotional, spiritual, and mental dis-ease. Nature has been my guiding force through my years of healing. When I witnessed the awe-inspiring recovery of the wounded maple, I distinctly heard the whisper in my ear: Humans have this ability as well.

What is our calling? Why are we here? The Truth is we are here to heal from the inside out. Then we can shine our glorious Light and love in greater proportions. Here is an astounding message that came through the ancient healing essence of Spikenard:

Nature is here to offer healing to those whose intention is healing. When you are faithful about your intention to use nature for your support, it is offered. Unconditional love is extended to everyone. Release old patterns of fear as creation does not come from a place of fear, only from the place of deep love. When fear is present, it is a reminder to stay in a space of trust. You will not be betrayed, EVER! Feel our unconditional love and know this Divine love is available to everyone. That is what is meant by the phrase "as above, so below." Feel Divine love come through your higher chakras and travel through you to your lower chakras. Above isn't a place, it is a higher frequency. Your invisible team is here to guide you to that existence. Trust and believe. It is as simple as that.

My hope and prayer for you is that you, too, will find ways to connect with nature and allow healing to emerge from within. As each one of us takes the time and effort to raise our inner frequency, our Light and love will change the world.

I leave you with a snippet from an interview between Krista Tippett and Robin Wall Kimmerer from the "On Being" podcast. Kimmerer asks the question, "Do you love the earth?" and then follows it with a deeper question, "Does the earth love you back?" Here are Kimmerer's thoughts:

> *"So it's a very challenging notion, but I bring it to the garden and think about the way that when we, as human people, demonstrate our love for one another, it is in ways that I find very much analogous to the way that the earth takes care of us...when we love somebody, we put their well-being at the top of a list and we want to feed them well...nurture them... teach them...bring beauty into their lives...make them comfortable safe and healthy. That's how I demonstrate love, in part, to my family and that's just what I feel in the garden, as the earth loves us back in beans and corn and strawberries... it's a really liberating idea to think that the earth could love us back, but it also opens the notion of reciprocity that with that love and regard from the earth comes a real deep responsibility."* (Tippett, 2016)

As you walk through life loving nature, may you feel the reciprocity of love from our Creator, loving you back and bringing the healing your soul desires for you.

"Forget not that the Earth likes to feel your bare feet and the winds long to play with your hair." Kahlil Gibran (Gibran, 2020)

Meditation

Acknowledging Your Truth

This meditation aligns your Throat Chakra, located in the center of the throat. This chakra involves the mouth, ears, jaw, throat and thyroid gland. It is the chakra for communication and self-expression. When in balance, you are able to speak clearly--always speaking from a place of inner Truth, feeling that you are listened to and honored for what you have to say, listening intently to what others have to say, valuing the opportunity to be present for another. You are able to express yourself creatively in kind, loving, clear ways.

When an imbalance occurs in this chakra, you may feel afraid to speak up and say what you want or feel, you may find yourself going along with others so you don't upset them, you may feel tightness in your throat or experience frequent sore throats when you refrain from speaking your Truth, or you may find that you talk nonstop, often feeling disconnected from your spoken words.

As we prepare for this meditation, let's begin by focusing on our breath, taking a slow, deep breath in and exhaling with a deep, audible sigh. On your next out-breath, release all that doesn't serve you in this moment … surrender to focusing on the breath and only the breath. On your next in-breath, notice how the breath feels in your throat … use the out-breath to sigh and release a little deeper. Relax your jaw … feel the muscles in your jaw and neck releasing.

Imagine a beautiful, rich blue light in front of you. With each breath, notice how that beautiful blue is expanding and becoming brighter and brighter. This brilliant blue light begins to move forward, and you follow. You find yourself at a bridge, and you begin to stroll across it with the blue light in the lead. Briefly looking back, you notice that all of the blocks to speaking your Truth are floating where you stood before you stepped onto the bridge ... people ... situations ... words left unsaid or spoken in anger. Releasing all attachments, you continue to follow the blue light. You reach the other side of the bridge, realizing the blue light is no longer in front of you but now is engulfing you in its blue radiance. A crowd of beings gathers around you ... they, too, are surrounded by this beautiful blue light ... everyone is peaceful ... everyone is communicating intently. ... You feel comfortable speaking with them as you notice how receptive they are as they listen to you. Feeling as if you belong in this space ... feeling a sense of joy ... feeling strong and courageous, you are able to clearly articulate what you want to say. You have found your place of Truth, and you embrace it with all of your being.

Smile softly to yourself as you begin to transition back to your space. Follow your normal breathing pattern as you gently bring yourself back into your body. Know that this radiant blue energy of Truth surrounds you, even now ... even as you step back into your life.

When you are ready, open your eyes, trusting in the Truth that lies deep within you.

Essential Oil Message
Review from Chapter 13

Truth

Clary Sage

You can enjoy the peaceful moments of nature at all times. You are trusting the guidance of the plants and trees more and more with each person you encounter. Be in that place at all times. Release the "not enough" mentality that creeps in to distract you. Think abundantly and trust the universe to do the rest. Listen to the still small voice within and follow guidance. You are always supported.

Davana

Stand in your power! Be clear and confident in your intention and it will manifest. There will be changes and it may be challenging, but all will go smoothly. Some of those you know will continue on their path with you and others may not. Know that you have given them exactly what they've needed at the time, and they will be led to their next step. You will find abundance coming to you easily and effortlessly in many ways--time for whatever your heart desires. You will receive abundance for your work. Your next best step is being revealed. Use the essences to support your efforts!

Grapefruit

The glass is half full. Remember this in all aspects of life, and find gratitude in all things. You have spent time wondering if some information is true and if the deliverers of this information are truly authentic. What does your heart say, not your head? If you believe in God, then believe with all of your heart. If you believe in Guides, then believe with all of your heart. If you believe in Angels and Plants and Trees, then believe with all of your heart. Doubting is a lower energy and not part of the upward spiral you desire in your life. It is possible to believe in all things with all of your heart. To thine own self be true! Remember to always follow and listen to your heart.

Spikenard

Nature is here to offer healing to those whose intention is healing. When you are faithful about your intention to use nature for your support, it is offered. Unconditional love is extended to everyone. Release old patterns of fear as creation does not come from a place of fear, only from the place of deep love. When fear is present, it is a reminder to stay in a space of trust. You will not be betrayed, EVER! Feel our unconditional love and know this Divine love is available to everyone. That is what is meant by the phrase "as above, so below." Feel Divine love come through your higher chakras and travel through you to your lower chakras. Above isn't a place, it is a higher frequency. Your invisible team is here to guide you to that existence. Trust and believe. It is as simple as that.

Appendix

Essential Oil Reference Guide

Below is a list of the essential oils that were mentioned throughout this book. My intention is to provide you with a brief summary of each essence's healing properties, with an emphasis on the emotional, mental, and spiritual aspects--those aspects that I highlighted throughout my meditation practice. I have also given a brief description of the physical healing aspects of each essence, its Latin name, and its country of origin. The two resources used to collect this information are: Wisdom of the Earth Essential Essences (oils) Book and Reference Guide (Kapp, 2015) and Aromatics International website (Aromatics International, 2020) at aromatics.com. When using essential oils, it is important to know the energetic qualities, as this determines if the essence may be cool or warm. I have listed the energy properties of Yin/Yin or Yin/Yang denoting first temperature (T) and then energetic (E), Yin = cool and Yang = warm. Please consult an experienced, educated aromatherapist for proper use of the essences.

DISCLAIMER:

The content of this reference list is intended for your educational and personal musings within the plant kingdom and should not be construed as medical advice. Please consult your qualified healthcare provider if you are in need of medical care and before making changes to your health regime. Any statements made or products mentioned are not intended to diagnose, treat, cure, or prevent any disease and have not been evaluated by the U.S. Food and Drug Administration. The plant realm cannot be patented; however, Mother Earth's Wisdom is available to all who honor, respect, and approach her with reverence.

Artemisia (Titepati)

Emotional/Mental/Spiritual: helps relax mind to surrender to the heart

Physical: helps drain upper colon mucus that links with lower respiratory dis-ease

General: Latin name: *Artemisia vulgaris*, Plant Part: Whole plant, Origin: Nepal, Energy: Yin(T)/Yin(E)

Black Pepper

Emotional/Mental/Spiritual: sharpens mental focus for more confidence/productivity, acceptance

Physical: increases circulation, great for joint or muscle pain, supports health of intestines, liver, pancreas

General: Latin name: *Piper nigrum*, Plant Part: Dried, crushed peppercorns, Origin: India, Energy: Yin(T)/Yang(E)

Cardamom Seed (Green)

Emotional/Mental/Spiritual: gentle heart opener, helps with mental fatigue, uplifting

Physical: increases circulation, helps to alleviate gas/heartburn and halitosis

General: Latin name: *Elettaria cardamomum*, Plant Part: Seeds, Origin: India, Energy: Yin(T)/Yang(E)

Cistus

Emotional/Mental/Spiritual: offers shelter and comfort after sudden distressing situations, helps bring closure to new and old emotional wounds

Physical: use for acute skincare, anti-infectious, queen to support immune system

General: Latin name: *Cistus iadaniferus*, Plant Part: Flowering tops, leaves, and branches, Origin: France/ Spain, Energy: Yin(T)/Yin(E)

Clary Sage

Emotional/Mental/Spiritual: brings a fresh outlook, soothes mind from negative emotional cycles, relaxing on all levels

Physical: regulates female and male reproductive system, supports and aids enlargement of prostate and menopause symptoms

General: Latin name: *Salvia sclarea*, Plant Part: Flowering tops of plant with leaves dried, Origin: France/ USA, Energy: Yin(T)/Yin(E)

Curcuma Zedoaria

Emotional/Mental/Spiritual: assists in seeing three level parallels, mind/body/spirit, is a Chi warmer

Physical: helps with pain from digestion in a gentle way, assists with sexual debility

General: Latin name: *Curcuma zedoaria*, Plant Part: Rhizomes, Origin: Nepal, Energy: Yin(T)/Yin(E)

Davana

Emotional/Mental/Spiritual: brings security to heart, calms anxiety and nervousness

Physical: assists with coughs and thick mucus, supports wound healing, coagulant

General: Latin name: *Artemisia pallens*, Plant Part: Pre-flowering plant with buds, Origin: India/Iraq, Energy: Yin(T)/Yin(E)

Fir Balsam

Emotional/Mental/Spiritual: supports keeping energy strong, creates movement, clears the air

Physical: allows breath to flow more easily, eases muscles and joints for movement, supports adrenals, lung support

General: Latin name: *Abies balsamea*, Plant Part: Chipped needles and bark, Origin: Canada, Energy: Yin(T)/Yang(E)

Goldenrod

Emotional/Mental/Spiritual: supports emotional and spiritual levels of the heart, reconnection, hypertension

Physical: supports balance with electromagnetic energy, supports healing of cardiovascular system

General: Latin name: *Solidago canadensis*, Plant Part: Flowering tops, Origin: Canada, Energy: Yin(T)/Yin(E)

Guaiacwood

Emotional/Mental/Spiritual: emotional support for grief, helps promote deep meditation and improves concentration

Physical: tightens loose skin, supports mature skin, assists with gout and inflammation

General: Latin name: *Guaiacum officinale. Guaiacum sanctum*, Plant Part: Tree heartwood, Origin: Paraguay, Energy: Yin(T)/Yin(E)

Himalayan Soti

Emotional/Mental/Spiritual: aura cleansing and strengthening, helps with emotional exhaustion, considered a passage essence

Physical: works well with eucalyptus and fir to support respiratory system

General: Latin name: *Cymbopogon* sp., Plant Part: Top parts, Origin: Nepal, Energy: Yin(T)/Yin(E)

Hyssop

Emotional/Mental/Spiritual: balances mood swings, inspires clarity and stillness, deeply spiritual

Physical: blood pressure stabilizer, adrenal stimulant, immune support, helps body release blocks to its natural health and comfort

General: Latin name: *Hyssopus officinalis* var. *decumbens*, Plant Part: Flowering tops, Origin: France, Energy: Yin(T)/Yin(E)

Laurel Leaf

Emotional/Mental/Spiritual: spiritual backbone to stand in one's Truth, bringer of courage, uplifting, alertness, cleanses stagnant energy

Physical: lymphatic support, supports recovery from Lyme disease, respiratory support

General: Latin name: *Laurus nobilis*, Plant Parts: Leaves, Origin: Bulgaria/Morocco, Energy: Yin(T)/Yin(E)

Lavender, Albanian

Emotional/Mental/Spiritual: gentle joy deva who opens doors of reconnection to Divine love, superb relaxant, bringer of incredible euphoric sensation

Physical: assists with respiratory congestion and infections, helps with insomnia

General: Latin name: *Lavendula augusti*, Plant Part: Flowering tops, Origin: Albania, Energy: Yin(T)/Yin(E)

Lemon, Cedro

Emotional/Mental/Spiritual: refreshing, positive can-do attitude, mental clarity

Physical: supports lymphatic system, anti-bacterial, disinfectant

General: Latin name: *Citrus limon,* Plant Part: Rind or peel of fresh juiced green lemons, Origin: Brazil, Energy: Yin(T)/Yang(E)

Marjoram (Sweet)

Emotional/Mental/Spiritual: calming, offers assurance in times of distress and encourages us to let go of what no longer serves us, helps accept change

Physical: thyroid balancer, supports body's natural detoxification, soothes bloated belly

General: Latin name: *Origanum majorana* m. *hortensis,* Plant Part: Flowering plant, Origin: Egypt, Energy: Yin(T)/Yin(E)

Mugwort

> **Emotional/Mental/Spiritual:** moves blocked energy to create new happy stories, helps with anxiety and nervousness, assists in relieving stress
>
> **Physical:** helps with respiratory infections, assists muscle spasms and tension
>
> **General:** Latin name: *Artemisia herba alba* Alpha-Thujone type, Plant Part: Whole plant, Origin: Morocco, Energy: Yin(T)/Yin(E)

Myrtle

> **Emotional/Mental/Spiritual:** soothes anger, fear, and despair; brings composure
>
> **Physical:** used for respiratory ailments, inflammation of bladder/kidneys/urethra, and congestion in lymph or blood vessels or veins
>
> **General:** Latin name: *Myrtus communis*, Plant Part: Branches, Origin: France/Morocco Energy: Yin(T)/Yang(E)

Niaouli

> **Emotional/Mental/Spiritual:** life enhancer, brings Earth's love
>
> **Physical:** anti-viral, supports overall health, lymphatic drainage, respiratory system
>
> **General:** Latin name: *Melaleuca quinquenervia viridiflora*, Plant Part: Leaves and twigs, Origin: Australia, Energy: Yin(T)/Yang(E)

Peppermint

> **Emotional/Mental/Spiritual:** stimulant, sharpens senses so you feel more alert and energized, helps promote clarity, creativity, and positiveness

> **Physical:** body coolant (used moderately), soothes upset tummy, calms headaches

> **General:** Latin name: *Mentha piperita*, Plant Part: Flowering tops and some stems, Origin: USA, Energy: Yin(T)/Yang balanced(E)

Pine, Ocean

> **Emotional/Mental/Spiritual:** queen of helping us go with ebb and flow of life, refreshes mind

> **Physical:** supports adrenals, helps alleviate UTI, addresses airborne bacteria

> **General:** Latin name: *Pinus pinaster*, Plant Part: Needles and bark, Origin: France, Energy: Yin(T)/Yin(E)

Ravintsara

> **Emotional/Mental/Spiritual:** Mother energy, promotes mind feeling sharp

> **Physical:** helps open breath, protects immune stimulant, calms heart palpitations

> **General:** Latin name: *Cinnamomum camphora*, Plant Part: Leaves and bark, Origin: Madagascar, Energy: Yin(T)/Yang(E)

Rosemary, Verbenone

> **Emotional/Mental/Spiritual:** helps mind feel clear yet relaxed, perfect for focusing, intimate harmonizer

Physical: restoring effects for skin and breathing, helps regulate endocrine system

General: Latin name: *Rosmarinus officinalis*, Plant Part: Flowering tops, Origin: France, Energy: Yin(T)/Yang(E)

Rosewood

Emotional/Mental/Spiritual: helps heal a broken heart, invites spiritual healing that permeates whole life

Physical: fortifies immune system, strengthens sexuality, antiviral/antibacterial

General: Latin name: *Aniba rosaeodora*, Plant Part: wood, Origin: sustainably sourced in Brazil, Energy: Yin(T)/Yin(E)

Sage, True

Emotional/Mental/Spiritual: gender balancer, resets to rhythm of the cosmos, facilitates reconnection to our oneness with Mother Earth

Physical: immune system stimulant, liver detox, helps rid of foreign molecules when a virus is present, excellent for sore throat

General: Latin name: *Salvia officinalis*, Plant Part: Flowering tops of plant, Origin: France, Energy: Yin(T)/Yin(E)

Spikenard

Emotional/Mental/Spiritual: helps tune in to hear things that are beyond our awareness, restores and increases dreams, opens door to deep spiritual thoughts

Physical: highly antiviral, used with wound healing

General: Latin name: *Nardostachys jatamansi*, Plant Part: Root and rhizomes, Origin: Nepal, Energy: Yin(T)/Yang(E)

Spruce, Blue

Emotional/Mental/Spiritual: grounding, helps you speak your Truth, meditation aid

Physical: immune system and respiratory support, thyroid balancer

General: Latin name: *Picea pungens*, Plant Part: Bark, branches and gum resin, Origin: Canada, Energy: Yin(T)/Yin(E)

Tamarack

Emotional/Mental/Spiritual: addresses shadow ego, shadow pride, and lack of compassion, assists with memory loss, fatigue and bi-polar disorder

Physical: aids coughs and colds and skin issues

General: Latin name: *Larix laricina*, Plant Part: Needles, Origin: Canada, Energy: Yin(T)/Yang(E)

Tansy, Wild

Emotional/Mental/Spiritual: deep, almost hypnotic effect, powerful for meditation, assists with channeling, considered Queen who shows us our strengths

Physical: powerful expectorant, antiviral and antiparasitic, anti-inflammatory

General: Latin name: *Tanacetum vulgare* (*chrysanthemum* v.), Plant Part: Whole flowering plant, Origin: USA, Energy: Yin(T)/Yang(E)

Violet, Absolute

Emotional/Mental/Spiritual: Queen of sensitivity, gentle protector when you are vulnerable, calming emotions, uplifting

Physical: soft nervine

General: Latin name: *Viola odorata*, Plant Part: Flowers and some leaves, Origin: France, Energy: Yin(T)/Yin(E)

Yarrow, Blue

Emotional/Mental/Spiritual: highly spiritual, opens heart/mind/spirit to cosmic energy and increases our awareness of intuition, calms difficult emotions, quiets uncomfortable issues

Physical: antiviral, supports sinusitis, rheumatoid arthritis, pain, gas, gout

General: Latin name: *Achillea millefolium* (*Achillea millefolium* var. *ligustica*), Plant Part: Flowering plant, Origin: Canada, Energy: Yin(T)/Yin(E)

Bibliography

Aetherna. (2018). Human Vibrational Frequencies List. *Aetherna Guild*, 1-3.

Aromatics International. (2020, December 13). *Shop Essential Oils*. Retrieved from aromatics.com: https://www.aromatics.com/collections/essential-oils

Chanel, A. (2013, January 03). *Vibrational Frequency and the Energetic Nature of Plant Prana*. Retrieved from antonikachanel.com: https://antonikachanel.com/blog/

Chardin, P. T. (2020, December 13). *Spiritual Awareness / Awakening Quotes*. Retrieved from Jesuitresource: https://www.xavier.edu/jesuitresource/online-resources/quote-archive1/spiritual-awareness-quotes

cummings, e. e. (2020, December 13). *e.e. cummings quotes*. Retrieved from BrainyQuote.com: https://www.brainyquote.com/quotes/e_e_cummings_161807

Einstein, A. (2020, December 12). *Albert Einstein Quotes*. Retrieved from BrainyQuotes: https://www.brainyquote.com/quotes/albert_einstein_106912

Emerson, R. W. (2020, December 13). *Ralph Waldo Emerson Quotes*. Retrieved from BrainyQuote.com: https://www.brainyquote.com/quotes/ralph_waldo_emerson_106883

Foster, J. (2020, December 13). *Art of Living Blog*. Retrieved from artofliving.com: https://theartofliving.com/you-are-enough-just-as-you-are/

Foundation for Inner Peace. (2007). *A Course in Miracles*. Mill Valley: Foundation for Inner Peace.

Gibran, K. (2020, December 13). *Kahlil Gibran Quotes*. Retrieved from BrainyQuote.com: https://www.brainyquote.com/quotes/khalil_gibran_106889

Gilbert, L. W. (2020, December 13). *L. Wlfe Gilbert Quotes*. Retrieved from BrainyQuote.com: https://www.brainyquote.com/quotes/l_wolfe_gilbert_404405

Hahn, T. N. (2002). *Be Free Where You Are*. Berkeley: Parallax Press.

Kapp, B. B. (2015). *Wisdom of the Earth Essential Essences Book and Reference Guide*. Bloomington: Balboa Press.

Larkin, W. K. (2016). *Growing the Positive Mind*. USA: Applied Neuroscience Press.

Macy, A. B. (2005). *Rilke's Book of Hours*. London: Penguin Books Ltd.

Mitchell, S. (2013). *Tao Te Ching: An Illustrated Journey*. London: Frances Lincoln Limited.

Monet, C. (2020, December 13). *Claude Monet Quotes*. Retrieved from BrainyQuote.comm: https://www.brainyquote.com/quotes/claude_monet_802612

Muir, J. (2020, December 13). *John Muir Quotes*. Retrieved from BrainyQuote.com: https://www.brainyquote.com/quotes/john_muir_108391

Myss, C. (2001). *Sacred Contracts*. New York: Harmony Books.

Nerval, G. d. (2020, December 13). *Gerard de Nerval Quotes*. Retrieved from BrainyQuotes.com: https://www.brainy-quote.com/quotes/gerard_de_nerval_166111

Paracelsus. (2020, December 13). *Paracelsus Quotes*. Retrieved from BrainyQuote.com: https://www.brainyquote.com/quotes/paracelsus_138349

Patel, N. (2013). GRATEFUL: A Song to the World [Recorded by Empty Hands Music]. 118 Countries.

Reber, S. (2013). *Raise Your Vibration*. North Charleston: CreateSpace Independent Publishing.

Richards, S. (2020, December 13). *Gratitude Quotes*. Retrieved from Goodreads.com: https://www.goodreads.com/quotes/tag/gratitude?page=8

Ruiz, D. M. (1997). *The Four Agreements*. San Rafael: Amber-Allen Publishing.

Rumi. (2020, December 13). *Rumi Quotes*. Retrieved from BrainyQuote.com: https://www.brainyquote.com/quotes/rumi_133529

Shakespeare, W. (2020, December 13). *William Shakespeare Quotes*. Retrieved from BrainyQuote.com: https://www. brainyquote.com/quotes/william_shakespeare_106907

Steiner, R. (2020, December 13). *Rudolph Steiner Quotes*. Retrieved from BrainyQuote.com: https://www.brainyquote. com/quotes/rudolf_steiner_202019

Tippett, K. (2016, February 25). *The Intelligence of Plants with Robin Wall Kimmerer*. Retrieved from onbeing.org: https://onbeing.org/programs/ robin-wall-kimmerer-the-intelligence-of-plants/

Walker, A. (2020, December 13). *Alice Walker Quotes*. Retrieved from BrainyQuote.com: https://www.brainyquote.com/ quotes/alice_walker_132291

Watts, A. W. (1974). *Cloud Hidden, Whereabouts Unknown.* New York City: Vintage Books. Retrieved from Good Reads: https://www.goodreads.com/quotes/7857834-you-didn-t-come-into-this-world-you-came-out-of

Wohlleben, P. (2016). *The Hidden Life of Trees.* Vancouver, BC: Greystone Books.

Wolfe, L. M. (1979). *John of the Mountains: The Unpublished Journals of John Muir.* Madison: University of Wisconsin Press.

Wright, F. L. (2020, December 13). *Frank Lloyd Wright Quotes*. Retrieved from Brainy Quotes: https://www.brainyquote. com/quotes/frank_lloyd_wright_127707

Further Reading Suggestions

To expand your understanding of the chakras:

Judith, A. (1993). *The Sevenfold Journey: Reclaiming Mind, Body & Spirit Through the Chakras.* Berkley: Crossing Press.

Mercier, P. (2007). *The Chakra Bible.* Toronto: Octopus Publishing Group.

Myss, C. (1996). *Anatomy of the Spirit.* New York: Three Rivers Press.

To expand your understanding of aromatherapy:

Kapp, B. (2008). *Wisdom of the Earth Speaks.* Sedona: Blue Moon Publishing.

Mojay, G. (1999). *Aromatherapy for Healing the Spirit.* Rochester: Healing Arts Press.

Olivera, C. (2019). *The Book of Annointing: A Divine Rebellious Act of Love.* Sedona: Cities of Light Publishing.

Zeck, R. (2014). *The Blossoming Heart.* Victoria: Aroma Tours

To expand your understanding of energy:

Grout, P. (2013). *E Squared.* Carlsbad: Hay House Publishing.

Rand, W. (2005). *The Reiki Touch Workbook.* Boulder: Sounds True

Stein, D. (1995). *Essential Reiki.* New York: Crossing Press.

About the Author

Nancy Zick has a deep reverence and passion for the natural world and the interconnectedness of all life forms. Through her massage practice and yoga classes, she offers her clients/students the opportunity to experience nature through aromatherapy and meditation. Her personal healing journey has included many holistic modalities: craniosacral therapy, massage, aromatherapy, acupuncture, polarity therapy, Feldenkrais, crystal healing, and Shamanic work. She facilitates women's retreats on her beloved island of Andros, Bahamas and also local day-retreats in Southeast Wisconsin, USA. She embraces a contemplative practice and believes in the mystic approach to her spiritual life, embracing the Truth of many spiritual paths: we are all one and created to love above all else. She and her husband currently live in Southeast Wisconsin.